MASTERING ARTISTIC DESIGN

PHOTOSHOP 7

D0521783

Kyoung-hoon Lee and Dong-mi Kim

Photoshop 7: Mastering Artistic Design

Credits: Senior Editor, Mark Garvey; Production Editor, Rodney A. Wilson; Technical Editors, Dave Huss, Kate Binder; Cover Design and Interior Design and Layout, Chad Planner, Pop Design Works.

Publisher: Andy Shafran

Technology and the Internet are constantly changing; due to the lapse of time between the writing and distribution of this book, some aspects might be out of date. Accordingly, the author and publisher assume no responsibility for actions taken by readers based upon the contents of this book.

Library of Congress Catalog Number: 2002107568

ISBN 1-929685-70-X

5 4 3 2 1

Educational facilities, companies, and organizations interested in multiple copies or licensing of this book should contact the publisher for quantity discount information. Training manuals, CD-ROMs, and portions of this book are also available individually or can be tailored for specific needs.

Muska & Lipman Publishing
2645 Erie Avenue, Suite 41
Cincinnati, Ohio 45208

www.muskalipman.com

publisher@muskalipman.com

Photoshop 7:
Mastering Artistic Design

Photoshop 7: Mastering Artistic Design

CD-ROM Organization

The CD-ROM

The supplementary CD-ROM that accompanies this book contains all of the source elements used to create the images found in this book.

Source Data

All example sources and image files needed are contained in this CD-ROM.

/Project_01 : (13 files)
/Project_02 : (15 files)
/Project_03 : (9 files)
/Project_04 : (12 files)
/Project_05 : (12 files)
/Project_06 : (5 files)
/Project_07 : (10 files)
/Project_08 : (3 files)
/Project_09 : (10 files)
/Project_10 : (6 files)
/Project_11 : (21 files)
/Project_12 : (4 files)
/Project_13 : (1 file)
/Project_14 : (2 files)
/Project_15 : (2 files)
/Project_16 : (7 files)
/Project_17 : (8 files)

Artwork

Includes the finished images made in the examples.

Project_01.tif - Project_17.tif (17 files)

Project 5
96

Project 6
112

Project 7
134

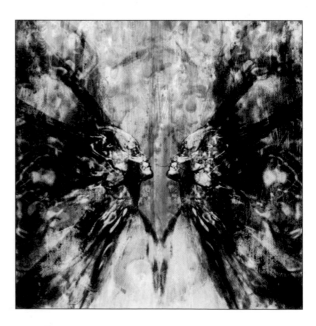

Project 8
156

Project 1

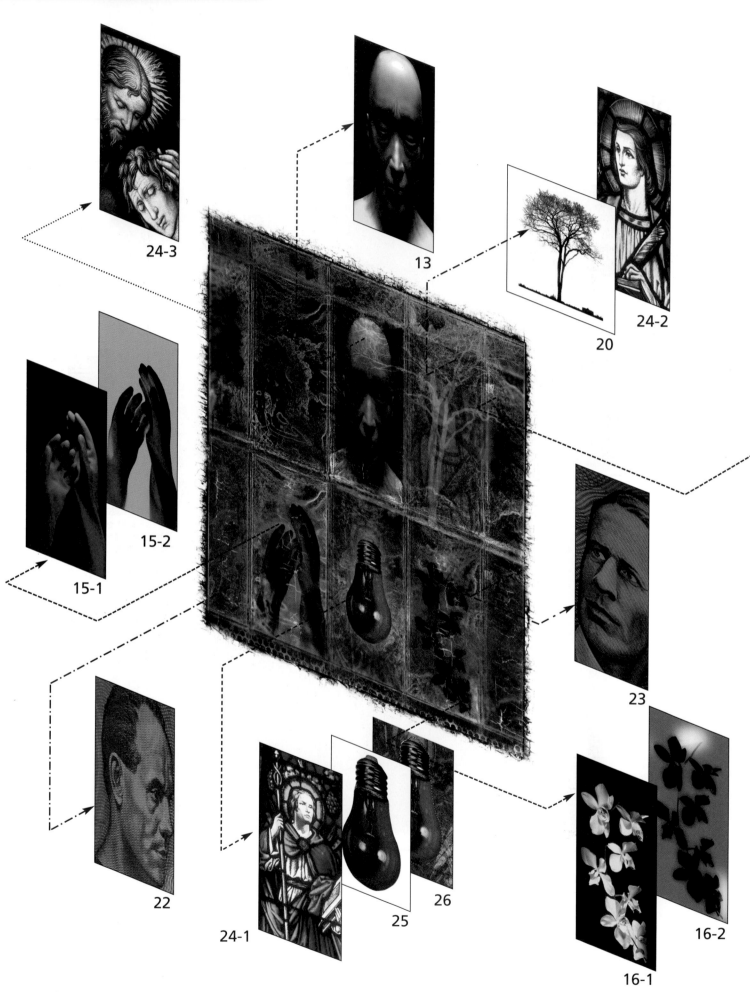

24-3

13

24-2

20

15-2

15-1

23

22

24-1

25

26

16-2

16-1

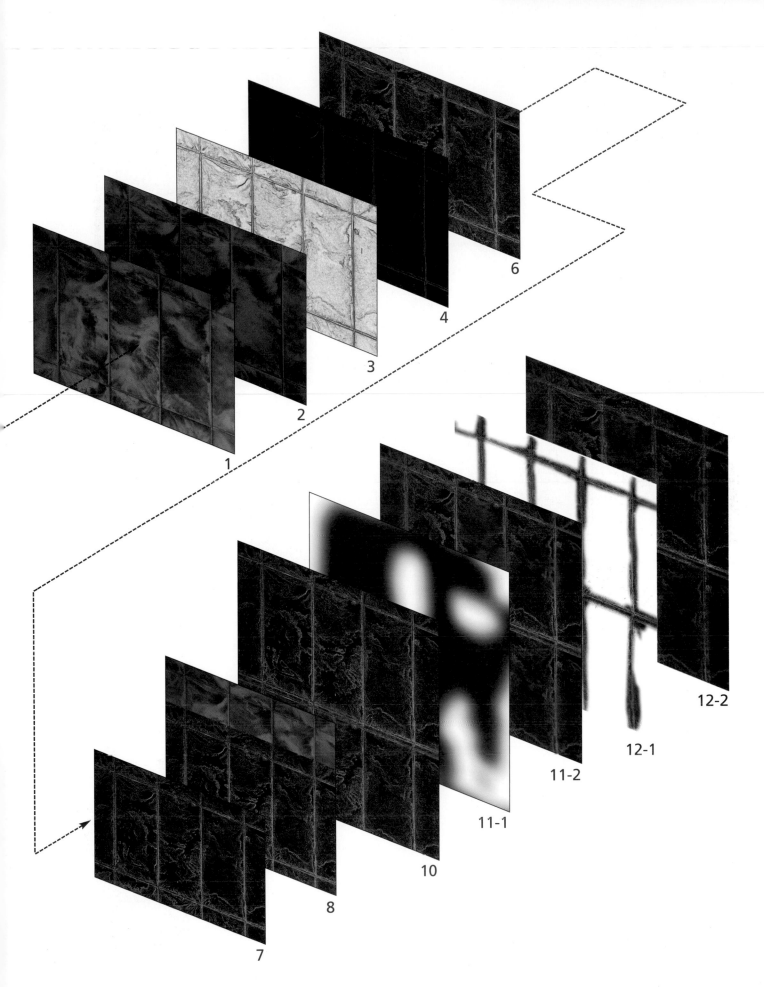

1

2

3

4

6

7

8

10

11-1

11-2

12-1

12-2

Step 1

Open the texture file that will be used as the background ("Background"). Duplicate the Background layer. The original layer is named "Background;" name the new layer "Background 2." Click to activate "Background 2."

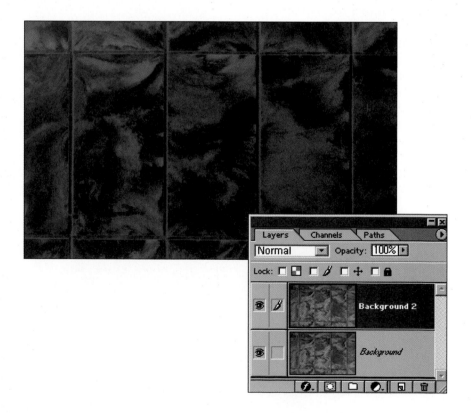

Step 2

Choose Image > Adjustment > Invert to invert the image's colors. Having made a copy of the image on a new layer allows us to experiment on the "Background 2" layer while preserving the original image on the "Background" layer.

STEP 3

Choose Filter > Stylize > Find Edges to apply a marbleized texture to the layer.

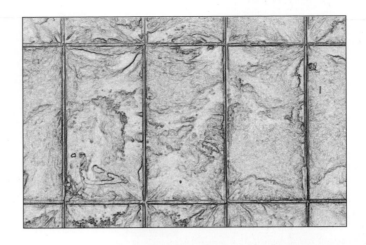

STEP 4

Invert the image again.

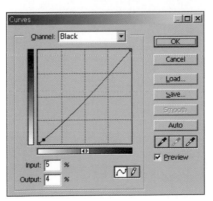

STEP 5

Choose Image > Adjustment > Curves to change the colors of each channel individually. We do this by adjusting the values until we arrive at the desired color. (For this project we have dragged the curves to adjust the values for cyan and black and then we have adjusted the overall curve for the image [CMYK] so the result is like the one shown on page 32.)

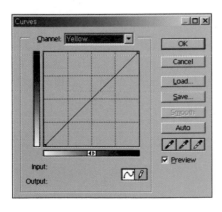

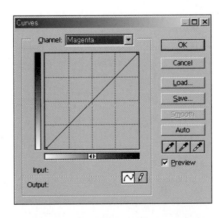

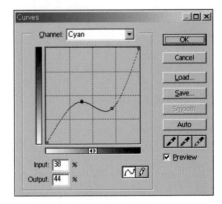

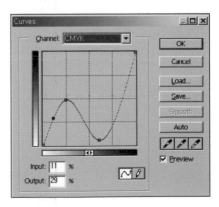

STEP 6

Here is the resulting
"Background 2" image after
adjusting the curves.

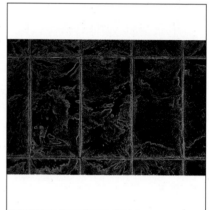

STEP 7

To provide room to enlarge
this image, we doubled the
height of the Canvas. Choose
Image > Canvas Size.

STEP 8

Holding down the Shift key,
drag the "Background 2" layer
to the bottom of the expanded
canvas. Drag the "Background
2" layer onto the Layers
palette's New Layer button to
create a third layer and name
the new layer "Background 3."

STEP 9

Use the Move tool to drag
"Background 3" to the top of
the canvas.

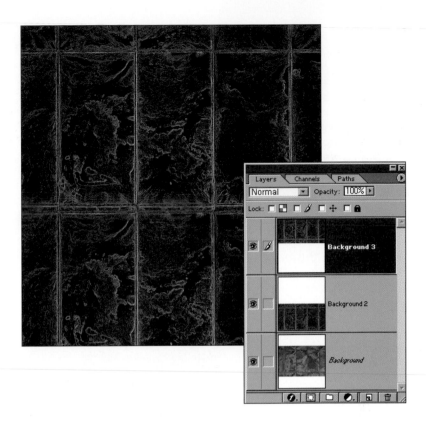

STEP 10

Precisely adjust the positions of "Background 2" and "Background 3" to create a seamless image as shown here and then choose Layer > Flatten Image to combine the two layers into one image. Use the Clone Stamp tool to eliminate the hard line between the two copies of the image. This combined image layer is named "Background." Finally, crop the image to show only the area you see here.

STEP 11

Before applying the blur, select the areas indicated in the alpha channel shown above. Next, feather the selection using a radius of about 30 pixels, and choose Select > Save Selection to create an alpha channel from the selection. In this way, you can load the selection later on. Apply the Gaussian Blur effect (Filter > Blur > Gaussian Blur, with a radius setting of about 5) to the selected areas inside the grid lines of the Background layer.

STEP 12

To emphasize the grid lines within the image, loosely select them as shown to the right using the Lasso tool and then choose Layer > New > Layer via Copy to create a new layer. Name this new layer "Background Grid Lines" and then set the blending mode to Overlay and the opacity to 100%. The background's grid lines appear slightly brighter and more intense. Now we are ready to work with this background. If the grid lines are too dark, brighten the layer by selecting Image > Adjustment > Brightness/Contrast.

STEP 13

Open the "Face" image. This image was created using Curious Labs'® Poser® program and retouched using Painter®. For further information, refer to "Working with Other Graphic Tools" in the back of this book.

STEP 14

Switch to the Move tool and drag the face image into the background image. Choose Edit > Free Transform and size the face so it fits into one of the "windows" in the background image. (Name the new layer "Face" and set its blending mode to Overlay with an opacity of 100%.)

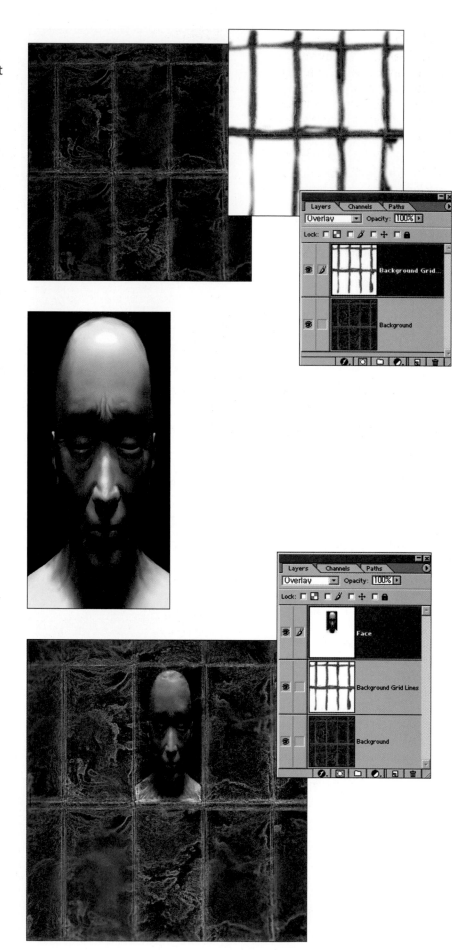

STEP 15

Now, open the "Rubber Gloves" image and drag it into the composite image. Choose Image > Adjustment > Invert to invert the glove image's colors. Name the new layer "Rubber Gloves" and set its blending mode to Overlay.

STEP 16

Open "Flower" and drag the image into the composite, then choose Image > Adjustment > Invert. Name the new layer "Flower."

STEP 17

Again, use the Overlay blending mode for the new layer and set its opacity to 100%.

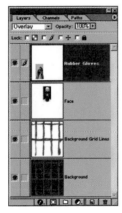

STEP 18

This image is a compilation of the images of the face, rubber gloves, and flowers.

STEP 19

Here is what the layers look like in the Layers palette.

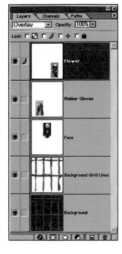

STEP 20

Open the "Tree" image and select the tree, excluding the white background, then paste it into your composite image. Invert the image.

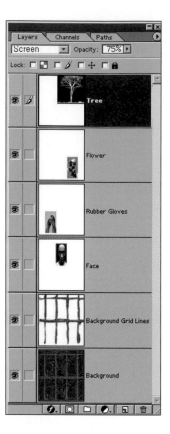

STEP 21

Name the new layer "Tree" and set the blending mode to Screen and the opacity to 75%. Here we see the resulting image.

STEP 22

Open "Man1," use the Move tool to drag the contents into the composite image, and name the new layer "Man 1." Situate it on the lower left of the composite image and set the blend mode of this layer to Luminosity. Then, adjust the opacity to 40%.

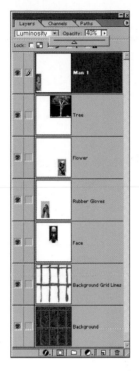

STEP 23

Open "Man2" and name the layer "Man 2." Set the blending mode of this layer to Luminosity and the opacity to 45%. This blending mode helps create an integrated effect for the composite image, and the lower opacity setting helps the image naturally blend into the background.

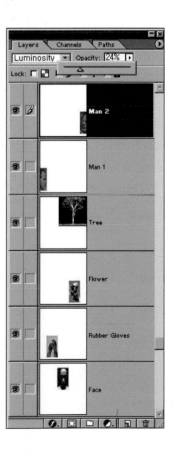

STEP 24

Open "Holy1," "Holy2," and "Holy3;" drag the images' contents into the composite image; and name the resulting layers "Holy 1," "Holy 2," and "Holy 3," respectively. The blending mode, opacity, and positioning of each of these layers are as shown on the right.

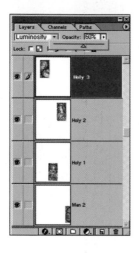

STEP 25

Open "Light," "Flowers," and "Eyes;" drag the images' contents into the composite image; and name the layers "Light," "Thorns," and "Eyes," respectively. The blending mode, opacity, and positioning of each of these layers are as shown on the right.

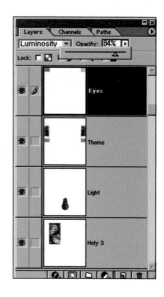

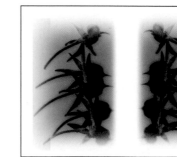

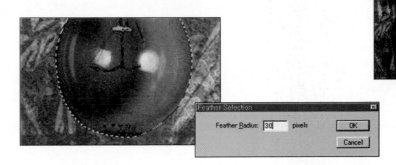

STEP 26

To brighten the "Light" background, create a new layer by clicking the Create New Layer button in the Layers palette, and then place the layer below the "Light" layer. Click on the "Light" layer while pressing [ctrl] to select the area around the light bulb.

STEP 27

Choose Select > Feather to soften the selection edges.

STEP 28

Choose Edit > Fill and fill the selection with white, then name the layer "Light Bulb Shadow."

STEP 29

Now enhance the glow of the light bulb by choosing Image > Adjustment > Hue/ Saturation. In the Hue/Saturation dialog box, click the Colorize checkbox and adjust the sliders as shown until a yellow color is obtained.

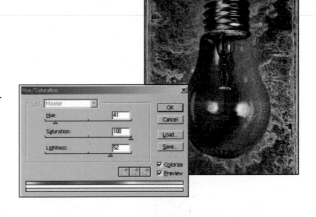

STEP 30

Save the file, then choose Layers > Flatten Image. Save the flattened image with a different name. Then, choose Image > Adjustment > Curves and adjust the brightness of the composite image to your liking.

Project 2

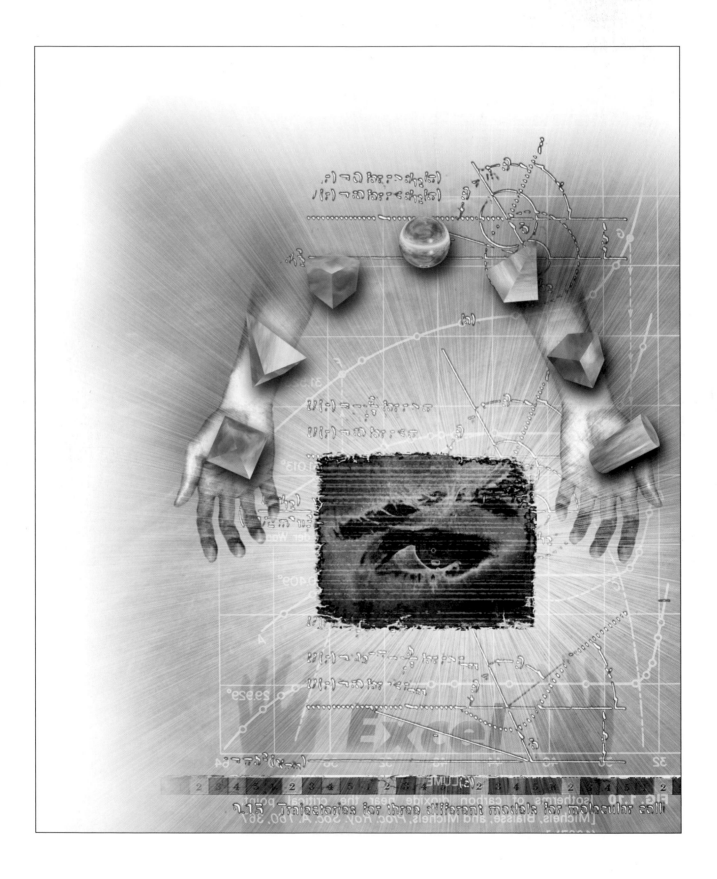

Project 2 Source Files

Background

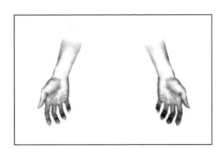

Hands

Eye

Figure 1

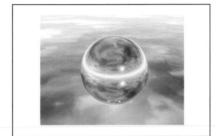

Figure 2

Figure 3

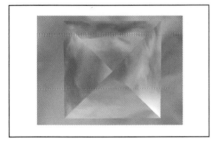

Figure 4

Figure 5

Figure 6

Figure 7

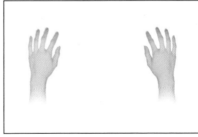

Hands 2

Graph

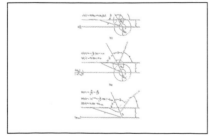

Formula

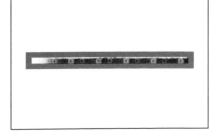

Numbers

Text

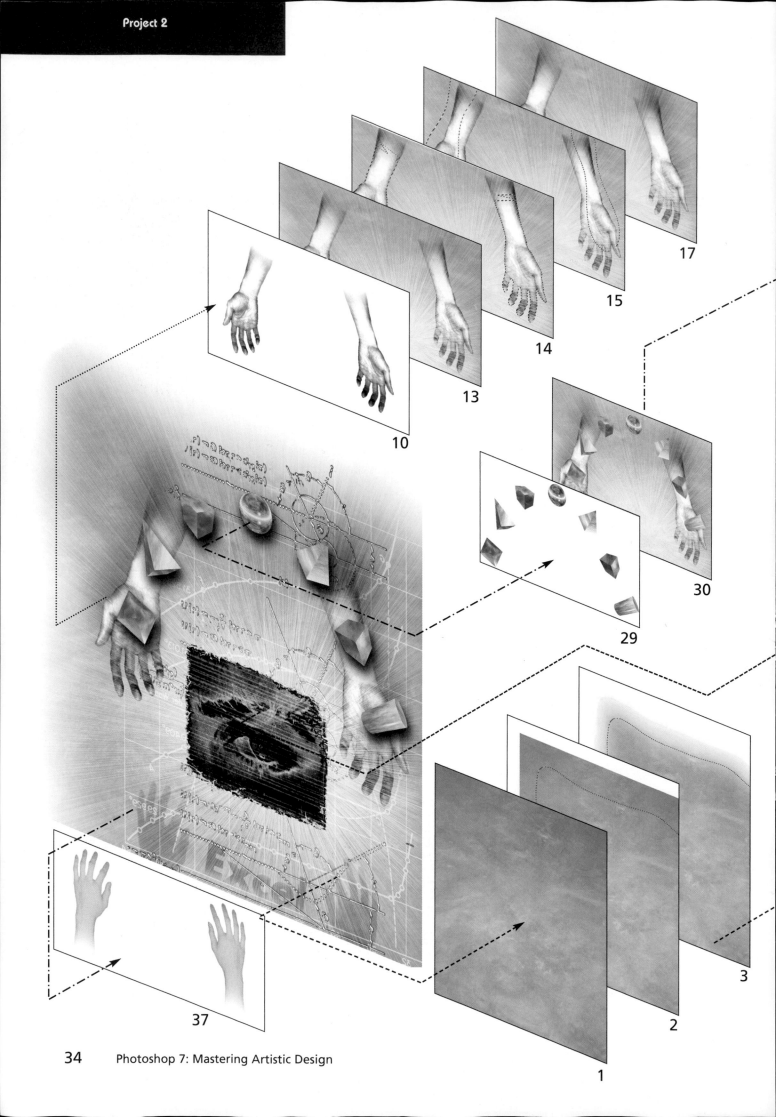

10

13

14

15

17

29

30

37

1

2

3

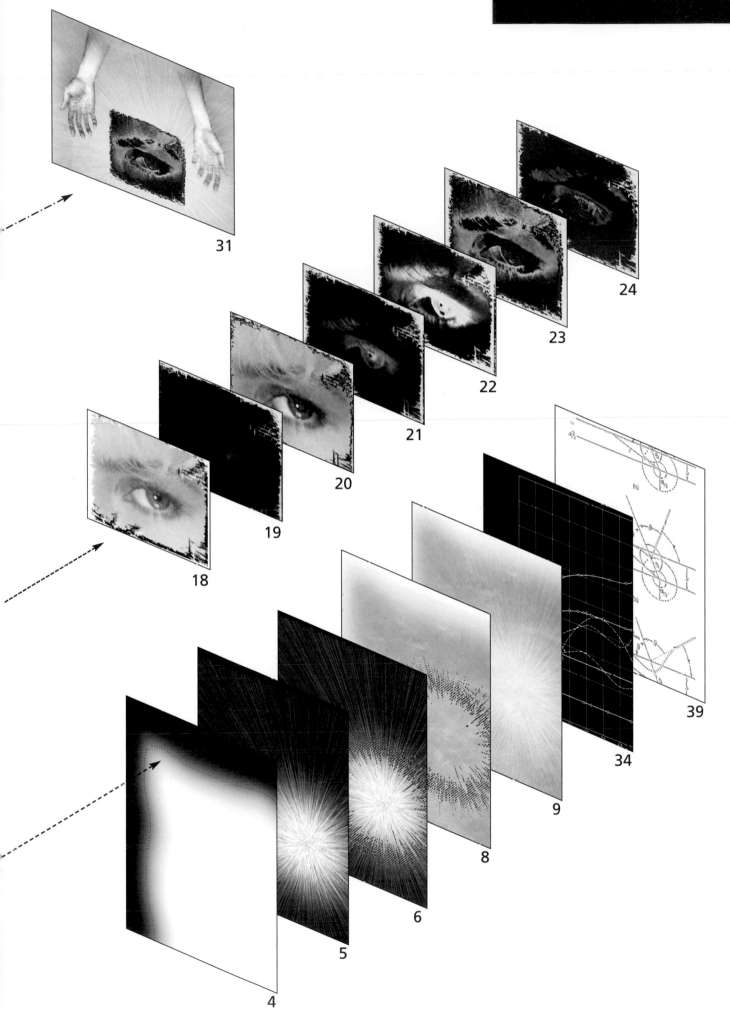

STEP 1

Open the texture image that will be used as the background

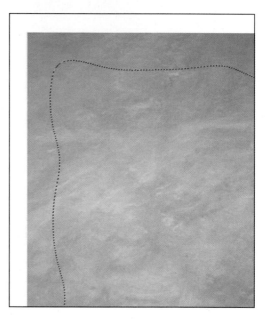

STEP 2

A layer mask must be applied to this layer to create a blank area around the background. To do so, double-click on the image's Background layer in the Layer Palette to turn it into a transparent layer. Name the new layer "Background" and choose Layer > Add Layer Mask > Reveal All to create the mask. Then use the Lasso tool to select the image as shown on the right. Depress X key to make the Background color black.

STEP 3

The effect is softened by choosing Select > Feather. Keep in mind that the greater this value, the greater the softened effect; in this case, set the Feather value to 100. Next, choose Select > Inverse and then press the [del] key to remove the outlying areas of the layer mask. Because the background color is set to black, the deleted area of the layer mask is filled with black. Where the mask is black, it hides the layer; where it's white, the layer's image shows through.

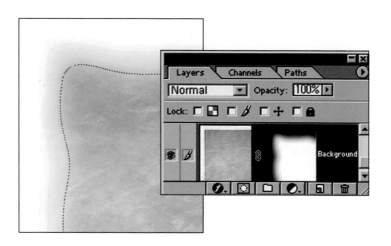

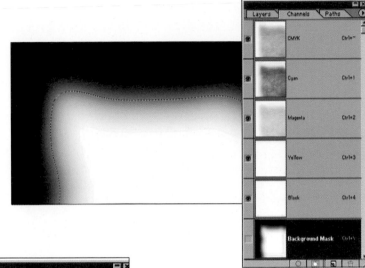

STEP 4

Display the Channels palette to
see the layer mask.

STEP 5

Create a new file—ours is 2677
pixels wide and 3246pixels
deep, in CMYK color mode.
Display the Channels palette
and click the Create New
Channel button at the bottom
of the palette. Name the new
channel "Light."

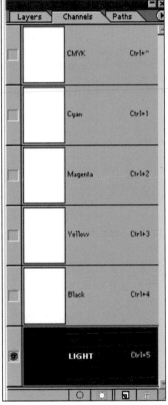

STEP 6

With the "Light" channel active, choose Filter >
Noise > Add Noise.

STEP 7
Choose Filter > Blur > Radial Blur.

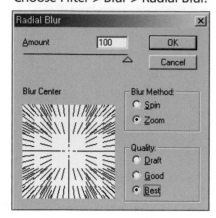

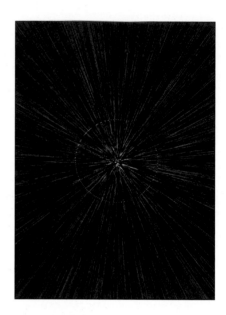

STEP 8
The background now consists of lines radiating from the center. You can emphasize them more by choosing Image > Adjustments > Brightness/ Contrast and adjusting the settings.

STEP 9
To add a highlight to the center of the image, use the Marquee tool to create a circular selection.

STEP 10
Choose Select > Feather and enter a value of 50 to soften the boundary of the selection marquee.

STEP 11
Choose Image > Adjustments > Brightness/ Contrast and drag the sliders until the area within the selection is almost white. This will create the effect of an explosion. Select all and use the Free Transform command to adjust the image's size and situate it as shown here on the right.

STEP 12

Activate the composite channel
and click on the Alpha 1 channel while pressing [ctrl]. The
bright areas will be activated
as the selection.

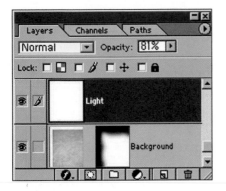

STEP 13

Click the Create New Layer button in the Layers palette and
name the new layer "Light."

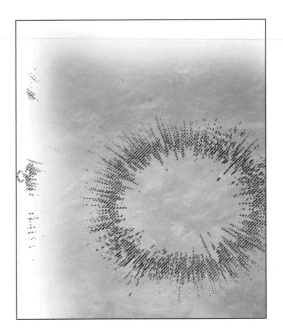

STEP 14

With the light burst selection still active, choose Edit >
Fill to fill the selection with white. Then set the new
layer to Normal blending mode at 81% opacity and
drop the selection.

STEP 15

The resulting "Light" layer is as
shown here.

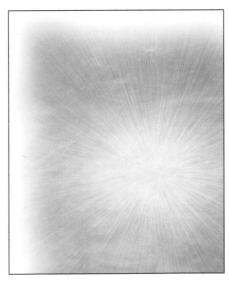

STEP 16

Open the "Hands" image. Select the hands, leaving behind their white background, and use the Move tool to drag the selected area into the composite image.

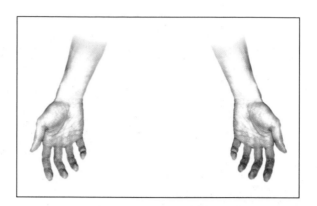

STEP 17

Name the new layer "Hands" and set it to Normal blending mode with an opacity setting of 82%.

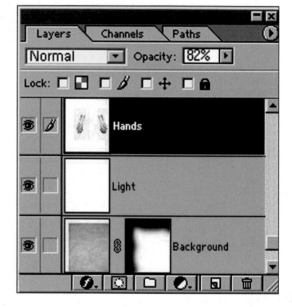

STEP 18

Move the "Hands" layer below the "Light" layer to create the effect of hands superimposed on the light.

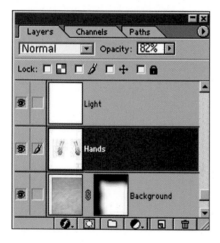

STEP 19

The completed image is as shown here.

STEP 20

The outline of the hands prevents it from blending well with the background; therefore, to soften the effect, we'll create a shadow. Press [ctrl] and click the "Hands" layer to select it as shown here. Now create a new layer and name it "Hands Shadow."

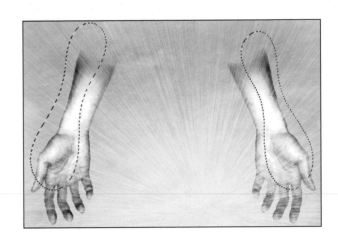

STEP 21

Choose Select > Modify > Expand (enter a value of 20) to enlarge the selected area, then choose Select > Feather (enter a value of 70) to soften this enlarged selection. This will soften the edges of the shadow we're about to create. We'll use the Feather command throughout this book to soften edges.

STEP 22

Choose Edit > Fill and fill the selection with black. We will need to brighten the color a bit. To do so, set the layer to the Luminosity blending mode and adjust the opacity to 34%.

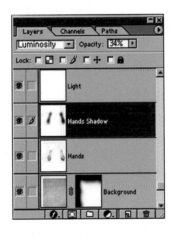

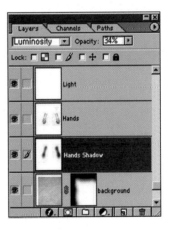

STEP 23

Place the shadow behind each hand. Because the "Hands Shadow" layer was created after the "Hands" layer, the shadow appears on top of the hands. To place the shadow behind the hands, drag the "Hands Shadow" layer below the "Hands" layer in the Layers palette. This is an important step in creating depth and dimension.

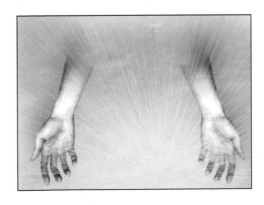

STEP 24

Next, open the "Eye" image. Use the Magic Wand to select the white areas of the image, invert the selection, and drag the image into the composite image using the Move tool. Size and position it as shown at right.

STEP 25

Name the resulting layer "Eye" and set it to the Difference blending mode with an opacity of 100%. We use the Difference blending mode to create a neon-like effect.

STEP 26

Click on the "Eye" layer and drag and drop it on the Create New Layer button. Rename the copied layer "Eye 2" and leave its blending mode and opacity the same. The two layers, both in Difference mode, form a high-contrast image.

STEP 27

The bright image of the eye does not blend well with the background. Therefore, choose Image > Adjustments > Curves to adjust the brightness of the "Eye 2" layer. (You'll find that you need to almost invert the curve to accomplish this.)

STEP 28

Adjust the CMYK values in the Curves dialog box until you get a color that emphasizes the eye and blends it well with the background.

STEP 29
Here is the resulting "Eye 2" image.

STEP 30
Revealing the "Eye 2" layer and hiding the original "Eye" layer creates the effect seen here. (Click the eye icon next to a layer to hide or reveal it.) The neon colors we want are created by the use of the Difference blending mode and the careful adjustment of the CMYK values.

STEP 31
Now we'll add slight slash marks to the image of the eye. First, you'll need to load the slash mark texture as a selection. The process for creating a channel that you can use to make the selection is explained in "Working with other Graphic Tools" in the back of this book. We used Procreate Painter®, but you can make a similar image using Photoshop's tools if you don't have Painter®.

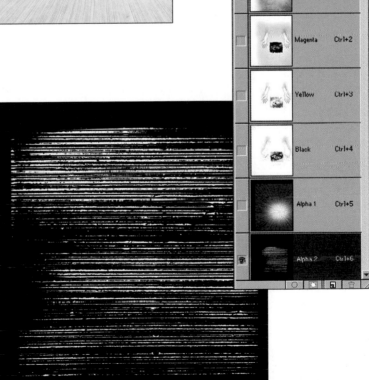

STEP 32

Clicking on the slash mark alpha channel while pressing [ctrl] creates a selection shaped like the white areas in the channel. With this selection active, click on the "Eye" layer while holding down Shift, Ctrl, and Alt to select only the areas of the slash marks that fall within the eye's boundaries. Click the Create New Layer button and name the new layer "Slash Mark Texture." Choose Edit > Fill to fill the selection with white.

STEP 33

Filling in the selection with white causes the slash marks to appear too bright. Adjust the brightness by setting the "Slash Mark Texture" layer to the Normal blending mode with an opacity of 50%.

STEP 34

We will add some figures created in Corel Bryce to the composite image. There are many 3D programs available, but we chose Bryce to create a natural surface in the rendered images; Bryce is especially good for creating images of nature such as mountains, rivers, and clouds. (Here, we chose figures that reflect the image of a cloudy sky. However, the choice is up to the user.) 3D primitives from any program that's familiar to you can be used here. (The creation of these figures in Bryce is explained in "Working with Other Graphic Tools" in the back of this book.)

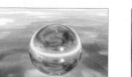

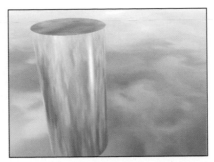

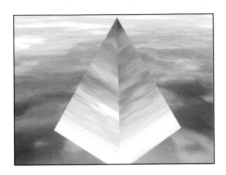

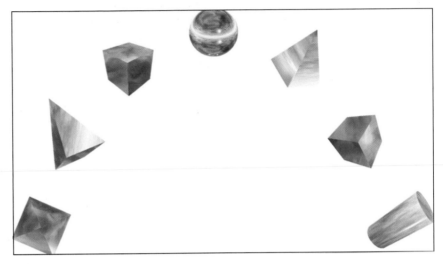

STEP 35

Select each figure, excluding its background; copy and paste it into the composite image. Then size and position the figures as seen here. This layout will be superimposed on top of the hands. A total of seven new layers were created in our version of this image.

STEP 36

The resulting layers are named "Figure 1," "Figure 2," "Figure 3," "Figure 4," "Figure 5," "Figure 6," and "Figure 7." After the figures are placed, activate the topmost object layer and choose Layer > Merge Down to make all the object layers into one layer. Rename this combined layer "Figure."

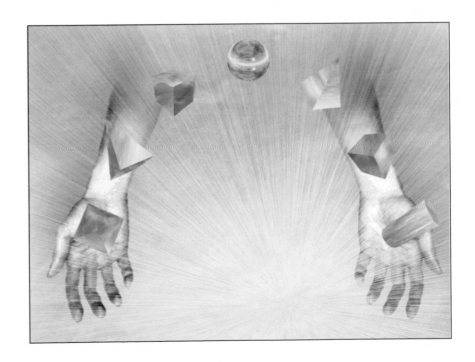

STEP 37

To create the effect of the figures suspended in air, a shadow must be applied to them. With the "Figure" layer active, choose Layer > Layer Style > Drop Shadow. Or, click the Add a Layer Style button located at the bottom of the Layers palette and choose the Drop Shadow option.

STEP 38

The Layer Style dialog box will appear. The values for shadow angle, intensity, and spread can be adjusted here.
•The desired effect is chosen in the Styles area at the left. A variety of other effects in addition to Drop Shadow can be found here.
•In the Structure area, the values for blending mode, opacity, angle, distance, spread, and size can be adjusted. Deactivating the Use Global Light option allows the user to apply styles with different lighting angles to each layer.
•The Quality value can be adjusted for Contour (transparency), Anti-aliasing (outline smoothness), and Noise (roughened shadow).

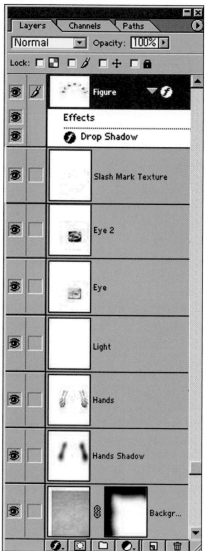

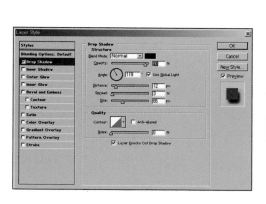

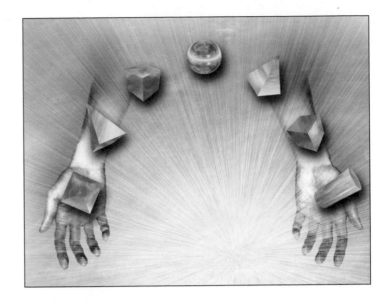

STEP 39

Here is the resulting image. The "Eye" layer has been hidden.

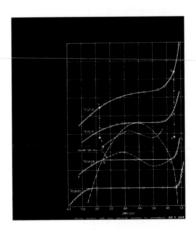

STEP 40

Open the "Graph" image and copy it. Switch back to the composite image, create a new alpha channel, and paste the graph into it. We'll use this image as the background for the hands and the figures.

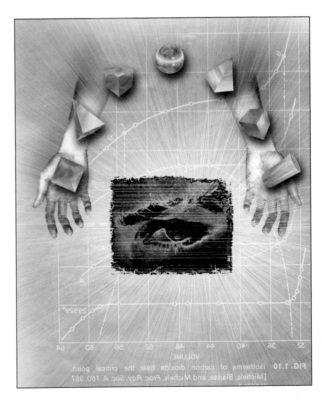

STEP 41

As described before, we'll use the new channel to create a layer. By creating the selection from an alpha channel, we can reselect it at any time. If file size is a problem, the selection process can be done in the channel and then after loading into the layer, the channel can be deleted. The procedure we're about the follow is similar to the creation of the "Light" layer in Steps 12, 13, and 14.

STEP 42

Create a new layer, then hold down [ctrl] as you click on the alpha channel that contains the graph image. Choose Edit > Fill to fill the selection with white, then name this new layer "Graph." Because this layer was created last, it appears at the top of the Layers palette and its pixels overlay those on layers lower down in the palette. This "Graph" layer will be used as the background, so move it below the "Hands," "Hands Shadow," and "Figure" layers so that it's immediately above the "Background" layer. Set the "Graph" layer to Normal blending mode and adjust its opacity to 70% to blend the image of the graph with the background.

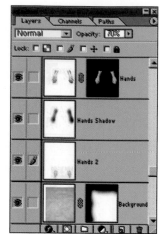

STEP 43

Now we'll add another image of hands that will be used as part of the background. Open the "Hands2" image, select the hands only (leaving the white background out of the selection), then copy the image and paste it into the composite image. Name the resulting layer "Hands 2."

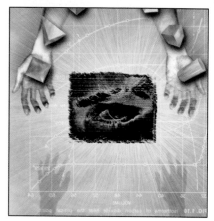

STEP 44

Set the "Hands 2" layer to the Difference blending mode and set its opacity at 17%, then move it below all the other layers except the "Background" layer. This will blend it into the background.

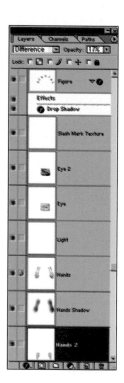

STEP 45

Now open the image of the physics formula, "Formula." (This image was created using channels; the process can be found in Project 11.) Use the Magic Wand to select the white areas of the image, then invert the selection and use the Move tool to drag it into the composite image. Name the newly created layer "Formula" and set it to Normal blending mode with an opacity of 100%, then move it below the "Hands Shadow" layer.

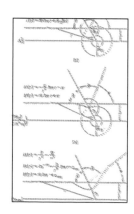

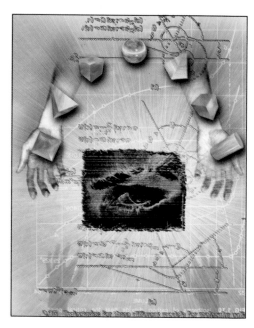

STEP 46

Now add the numbers that will be placed at the bottom of the image. Open the "Numbers" image, select the number strip, and use the Move tool to drag it into the composite image. Name the new layer "Numbers" and set it to Normal blending mode with an opacity of 94%.

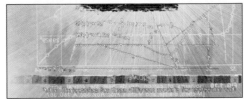

STEP 47

Finally, we'll add the "Excel" text image. Choose the Type tool and click in the image, then select a font and size and set the text color to white. Enter the text "Excel." The type is created on its own layer. Set the type layer's blending mode to Difference and its opacity to 14%. This creates a faintly dark effect. Move the text layer below the "Formula" layer.

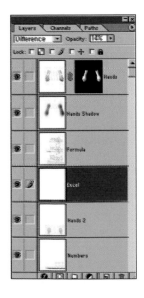

Project 3

Project 3 Source Files

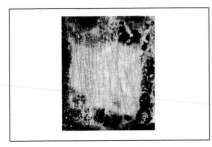

Background

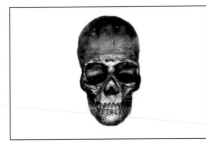

Head

Hand-R

Hand-L

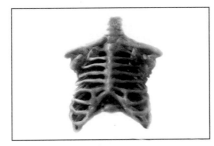

Rib Cage

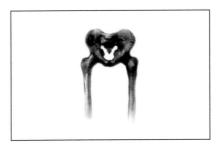

Pelvic Bone

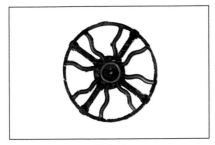

Object

Candle

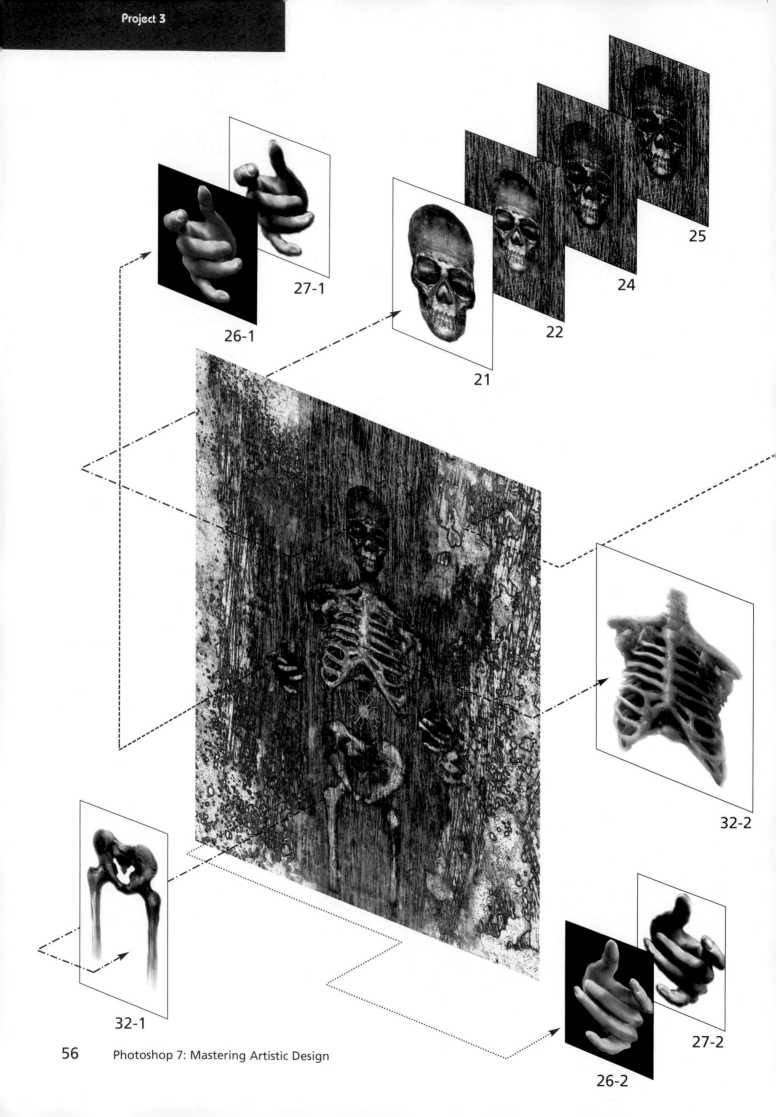

27-1

26-1

25

24

22

21

32-2

32-1

27-2

26-2

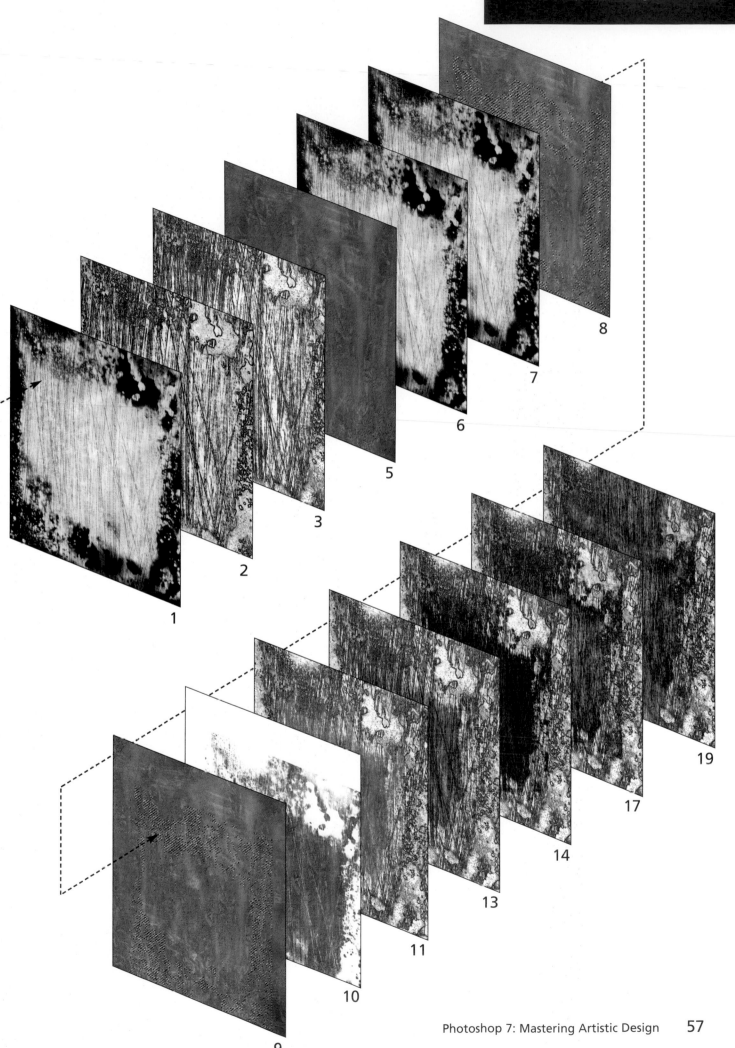

1

2

3

5

6

7

8

9

10

11

13

14

17

19

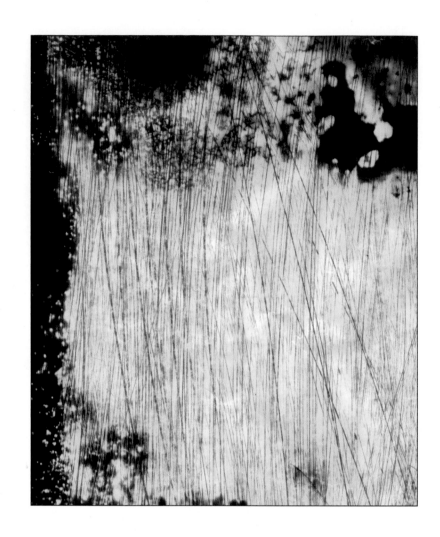

STEP 1

Open the "Background" texture image that will be used as the background. (Note: Work 3 was created using the RGB color mode throughout.)

STEP 2

Choose Filter > Stylize > Find Edges.

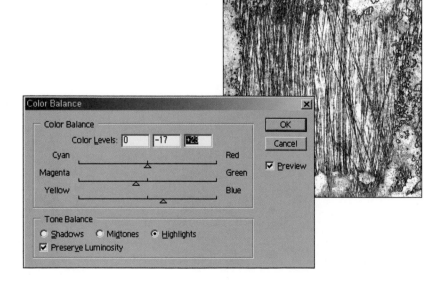

STEP 3

Adjust the color of the image by choosing Image > Adjustments > Color Balance and making settings as shown.

STEP 4

Save the file under a different name and close it, then reopen the texture file that was used as the basis for your colorized image. Copy the original image and close the file. (Closing the composite file means that we'll only have one file open at a time. This helps if you're low on RAM or hard disk space.)

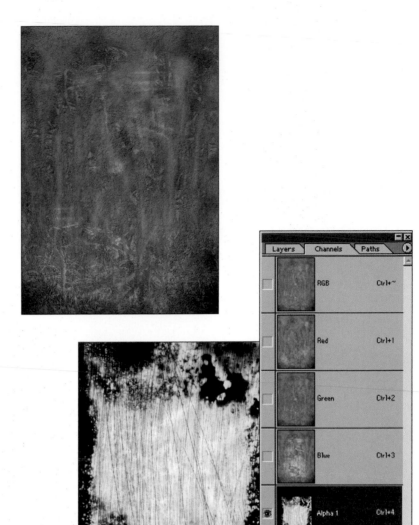

STEP 5

Open the "Scratch" image file. Now, we will use the original texture to create a frame that will be centered in the window.

STEP 6

Open the Channels palette. Create a new channel using the Create New Channel button and paste the copied texture.

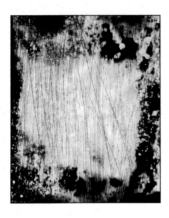

STEP 7

Choose Image > Adjustments > Brightness/ Contrast to deepen the image's shadows.

STEP 8

Adjust the size and position of the texture using the Free Transform command in the Edit menu. Then click on the channel while pressing [ctrl] to create a selection based on this channel.

STEP 9

After activating the composite RGB color channel, invert the selection by choosing Select > Inverse.

STEP 10

Press [del] to remove the areas of the image defined by the selection. A frame is created as shown here. Invert the selection frame again and copy its contents. Then close the file.

STEP 11

Reopen the composite file that you saved in Step 4, open the Layers palette, and paste the copied frame. This will create a new layer.

STEP 12

Name this new layer "Frame." Set the blending mode to Multiply and adjust the layer's opacity to 100%.

STEP 13

Because this channel was copied and pasted, a portion of the outline will remain. This portion can be selected using the Lasso tool and then removed by pressing the [del] key.

STEP 14

Duplicate the "Frame" layer and set the blending mode of the new layer to Difference with an opacity of 100%.

STEP 15

Name this layer that appears above the "Frame" layer "Frame 2."

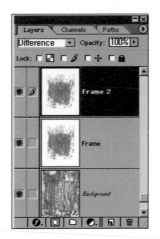

STEP 16

To blend the "Frame" and "Frame 2" layers with the "Background" layer, use features such as Hue/Saturation or Curves to adjust the color to your liking.

STEP 17

By following steps 12-16, you have superimposed this complementary small background over the "Background" layer.

STEP 18

Choose Layer > Flatten Image to merge the three layers into one "Background" layer.

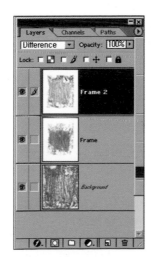

STEP 19

Switch to the Clone Stamp tool so that you can expand the area (from top to bottom) of the smaller green background.

STEP 20

First, adjust the Clone Stamp tool's opacity and brush size in the Options bar at the top of your screen. Then, hold down the [alt] key as you click in the area you want to copy. Click in the area where you want to place the copied pixels. Repeat as necessary to extend the green area to the top and bottom of the window.

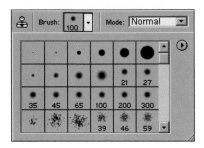

STEP 21

Open the "Head" image file.

STEP 22

Select the skull image, leaving behind the white background; copy and paste it into the composite image. Name the new layer "Head." Choose Edit > Free Transform so that you can size and position the skull as shown.

STEP 23

Duplicate the "Head" layer and name the new layer "Head 2." Set the blending mode of the "Head" layer to Difference with an opacity of 100% and the "Head 2" layer to Overlay with an opacity of 35%.

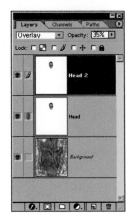

STEP 24

We can see the image of the skull superimposed on the background.

STEP 25

We have created the effect of a skull, which roughly protrudes from the background. The texture of the background will also be applied to the skull.

STEP 26

Open the next two object images, "Hand-R" and "Hand-L," and delete the black background from each image.

STEP 27

Adjust the contrast in the hand images by choosing Image > Adjustments > Brightness/Contrast.

STEP 28

Copy and paste the hands into the composite image, position them as shown, and merge the two new layers into one; name it "Hands." Copy this layer and name the new layer "Hands 2."

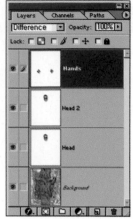

STEP 29

Set the blending mode and opacity of the "Hands" layer to the same parameters as the "Head" layer (Difference, 100%). The "Hands 2" layer, however, is set to the Overlay mode with an opacity of 85%.

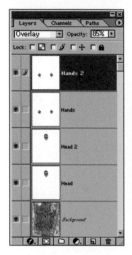

STEP 30

The "Hands" layer is seen here superimposed on the background.

STEP 31

In addition, the small, green background can be selected using the Lasso tool, copied, pasted, and placed below the layers of the object images to create a darker texture quality. Due to the limitations of the Adjustments commands in the Image menu, this is a good option.

STEP 32

Excluding their respective backgrounds, copy two more object images, "Pelvic Bone" and "Ribcage," and paste them into the composite image. Size and position them as shown.

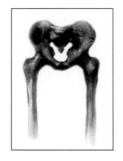
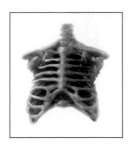

STEP 33

In this step, we do not make one copy of the image as we have done before. First, activate the "Ribcage" image and make two copies for a total of three identical layers. Name the layers "Ribcage 1," "Ribcage 2," and "Ribcage 3" and set their blending modes to Difference with an opacity of 100%. For a more natural image, adjust the hue/saturation, curves, and brightness/contrast for each of these layers.

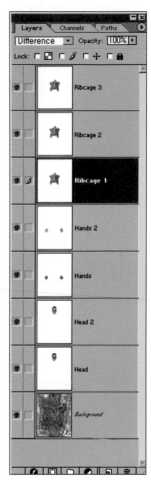

STEP 34

The skull and hands were purposely made to create the effect of roughly protruding from the background, and the ribcage and pelvic bone, while maintaining the quality of the background, were created to emphasize their individual characteristics.

STEP 35

After activating the "Pelvic Bone" layer, the process is the same as Step 33. However, the third pelvic bone layer, "Pelvic Bone 3," should be set to Overlay mode with an opacity of 100. This is to differentiate it slightly from the "Ribcage" image.

STEP 36

This is the completed image thus far. The important point here is that the brightness /contrast, curves, and hue/saturation were manipulated separately for each pelvic bone layer to emphasize the mood of the background. It is essential to practice this step repeatedly. In general, when using the Difference and Overlay modes to create a contrast between the background and the object images, you'll get better results by using grayscale objects.

STEP 37

Now load the image that will be inserted between the ribcage and pelvic bone, "Object." Copy the object, without its white background, and paste it into the composite image. Size and position it as shown.

STEP 38

Set the new layer to Screen mode and adjust its hue and saturation until the desired color is achieved.

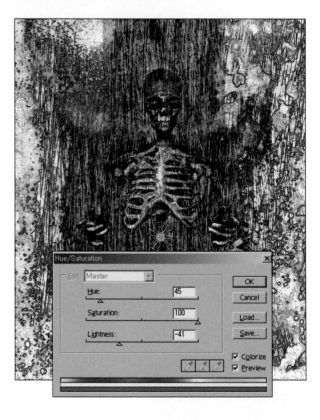

STEP 39

Name the newly created layer "Layer 4."

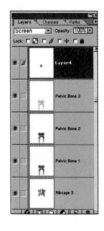

STEP 40

Open the "Candle" image. Choose Image > Mode > Grayscale. In the Channels palette, click on the "Gray" channel while pressing [ctrl] to create a selection based on the channel. Copy the contents of the selection.

STEP 41
Return to the composite file.

STEP 42
Paste the copied image.

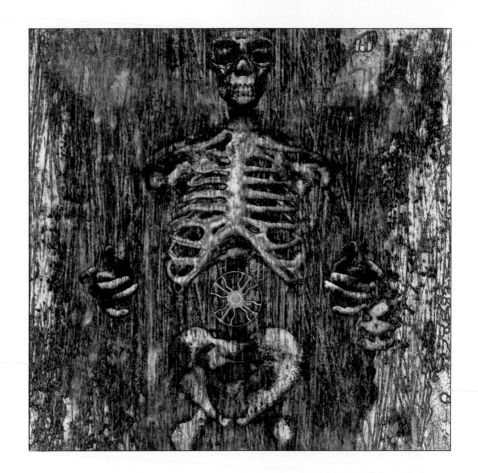

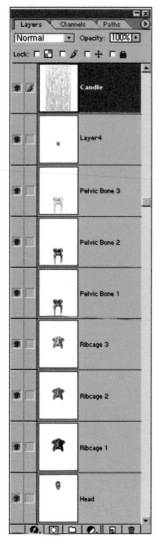

STEP 43
Name the new layer "Candle."

STEP 44
Adjust the "Candle" layer's opacity to your liking. The dripping candle image is superimposed on the background to complete the image.

Project 4

Project 4 Source Files

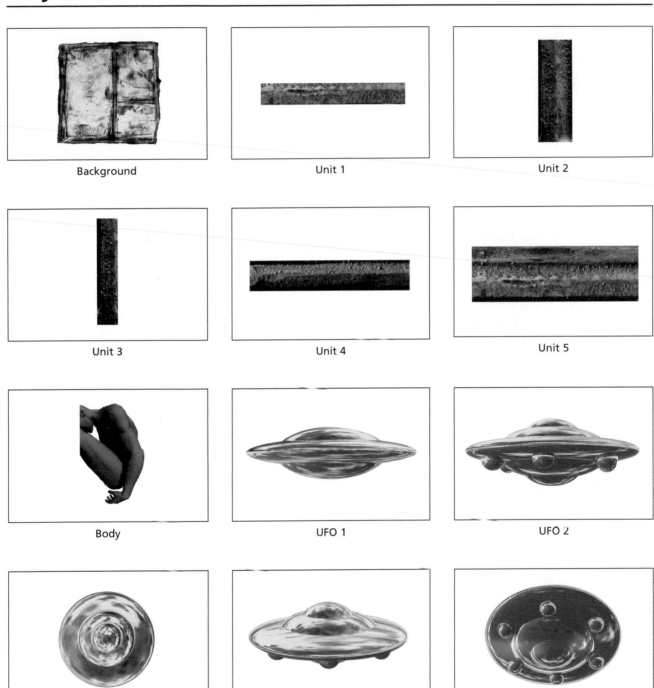

Background

Unit 1

Unit 2

Unit 3

Unit 4

Unit 5

Body

UFO 1

UFO 2

UFO 3

UFO 4

UFO 5

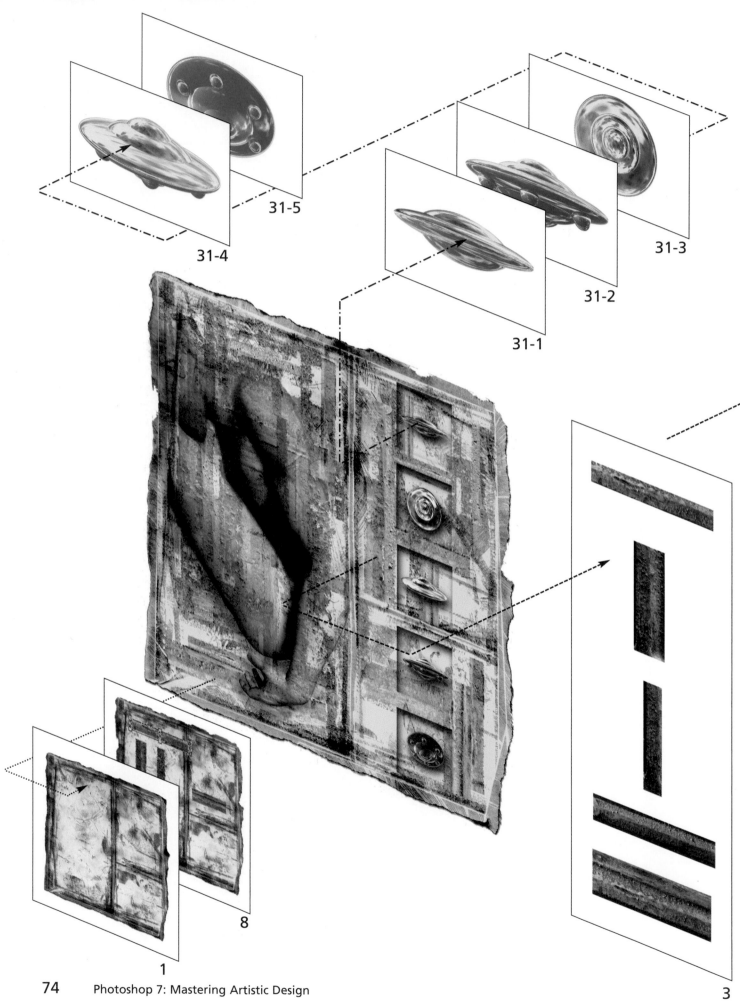

31-5

31-4

31-3

31-2

31-1

8

1

3

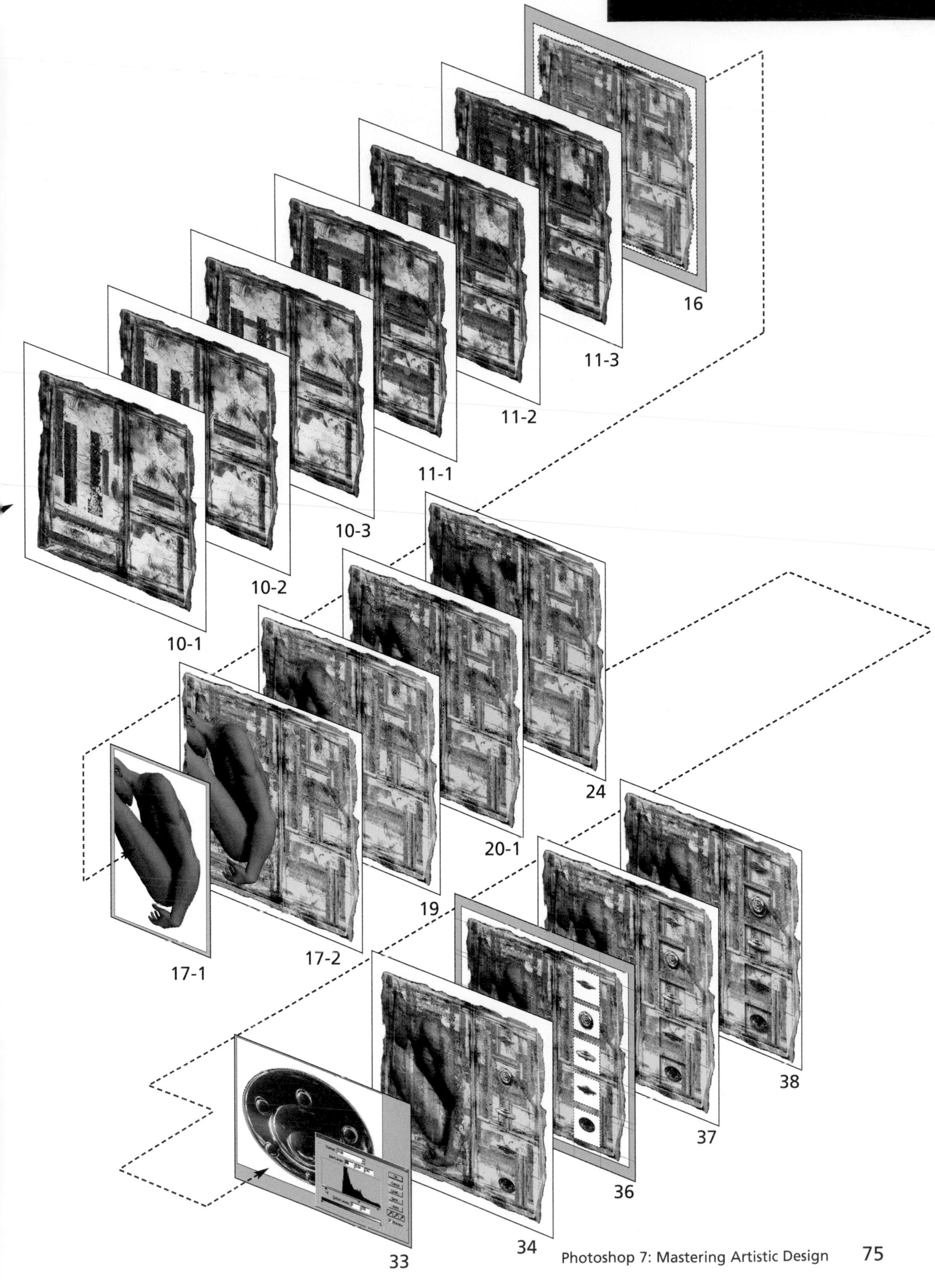

16

11-3

11-2

11-1

10-3

10-2

10-1

24

20-1

19

17-1

17-2

38

37

36

34

33

STEP 1

Open the manually drawn image that will be used as the background. This image is a wood print using acrylic paints that was scanned into the computer.

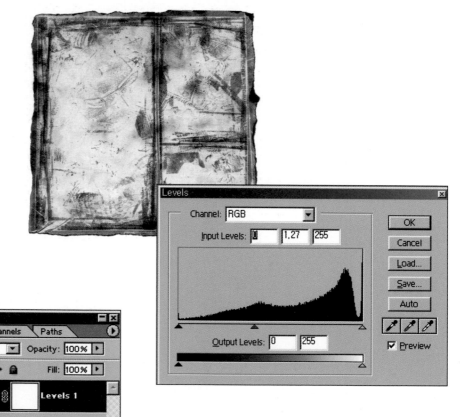

STEP 2

Adjust the brightness of the image if it appears overly dark. In order to adjust the brightness at any time while working, use a Levels adjustment layer. Click the Adjustment Layer button at the bottom of the Layers palette and choose Levels. Adjust the values in this dialog box as shown here.

STEP 3

As we saw in the preview of the completed image that was shown earlier, we are trying to create a background that appears to be made up of wooden fragments. In other words, we are trying to create a large background texture that is made up of small individual units. Although this looks complex, if we keep in mind that this step uses the Free Transform function to slightly alter the length and width of different layers and adds a few blending modes to create an aged effect, it is not that difficult. First of all, we see here the images that will be needed for the background texture. We will call these "unit images." These unit images are actually scanned photographs of an old bronze street lamp.

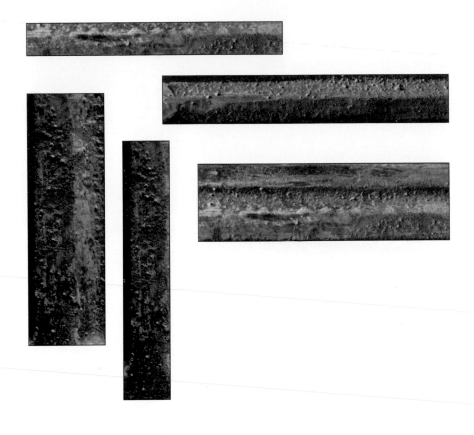

STEP 4

Open Unit_1 through Unit_5. In order to make these images appear old and frayed, we created a bumpy, rather than a straight, outline. Choosing the Lasso tool from the Toolbox, we created a rough outline of the image. After a rough silhouette is drawn, choose Select > Inverse so that the interior of the image is selected.

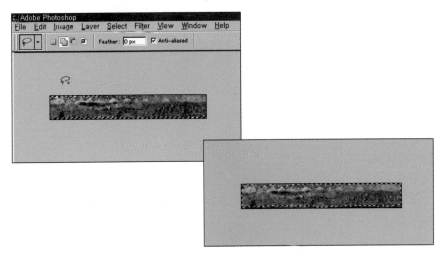

STEP 5

To create a rougher outline, choose the Magic Wand tool from the Toolbox and select portions of the image while alternately pressing the Shift and Alt keys. (Mac users use the Shift and Option keys.) The Tolerance level for the Magic Wand tool should be set at a low 10-20.

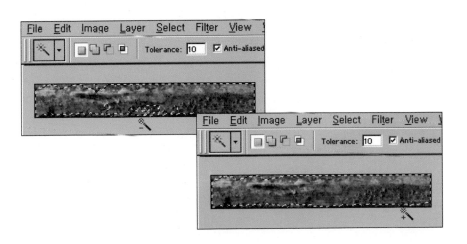

STEP 6

Once the touch-ups have been made to the unit images, copy each of these images, one at a time, into the background file, while the respective image files are still open.

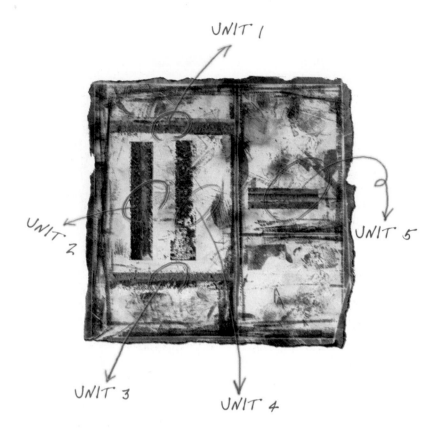

UNIT 1
UNIT 2
UNIT 5
UNIT 3
UNIT 4

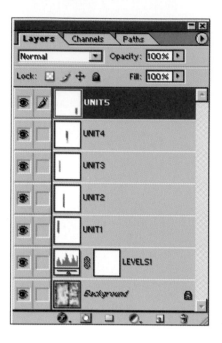

STEP 7

The user will find that as the unit images are repeatedly blended in the next few steps, many layers will appear, and it will be very difficult to remember the names of each of them and to find them to complete the work. It will be much easier if each of the five unit images is put into a layer set. Click the Create a New Set button at the bottom of the Layers palette to create a different layer set for each of the five unit images. Then, drag each of the unit images to its respective set. Then right-click or [ctrl]+click on each layer set and choose Layer Set Properties to specify the name of each layer.

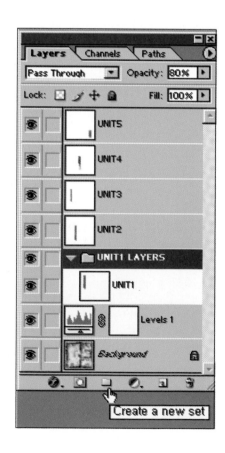

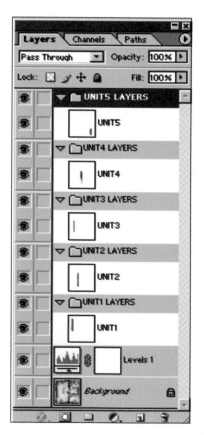

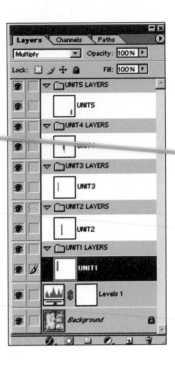

STEP 8

We will now overlap the five images to create the background texture. Rather than merely changing the direction of the images and arranging them on the background, it is important that the length and width of each image be adjusted using the Free Transform command ([ctrl]+[t] or Command +[t]) while the Opacity value is adjusted at the same time. For a smooth finish, the Multiply Mode is used at 85-88%. Let's start by blending the "Unit 1" image from the "Unit 1 Layers" set. Taking care that the image does not get too big, use the Free Transform command ([ctrl]+[t]) to appropriately position the image.

STEP 9

As a side note, the number of unit images that have been adjusted to create the background texture shown here is about 60. To create more diversity, the unit images from each set can be copied into other unit sets and blended to create unique images. However, don't use an unnecessarily high number of layers. Let's take a closer look at the way we adjusted the image size and direction in order to save disk space.

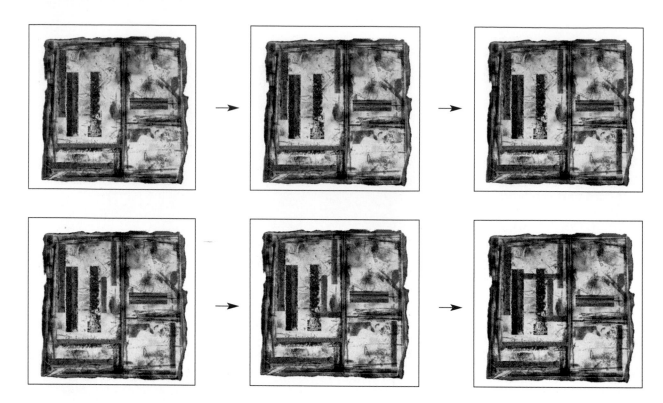

STEP 10

Here is an example of the continuous duplication and rearrangement of the "Unit 1" image from the "Unit 1 Layers" set.

STEP 11

Here are several steps in the duplication, adjustment, and alignment of the "Unit 2" image.

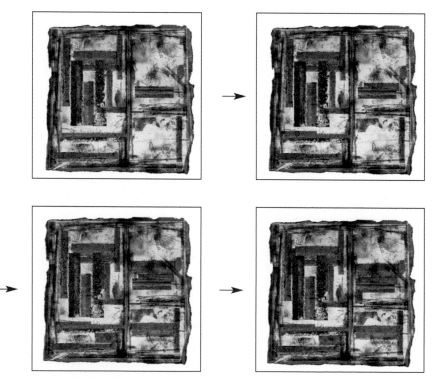

STEP 12

A rough background texture is complete. We now need to brighten up the overly dark image. Use an adjustment layer to create a layer that includes the Levels function. This adjustment layer feature is very convenient for allowing the user to make adjustments at any time while working.

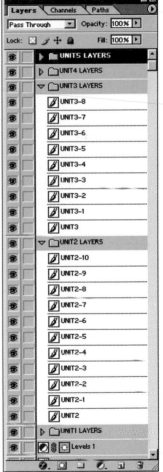

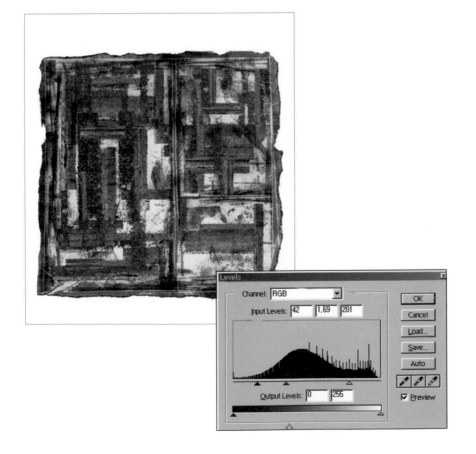

STEP 13

As we saw in the preview of the completed image, the black and white background images will be changed to brown. We do this by using a Hue/Saturation adjustment layer.

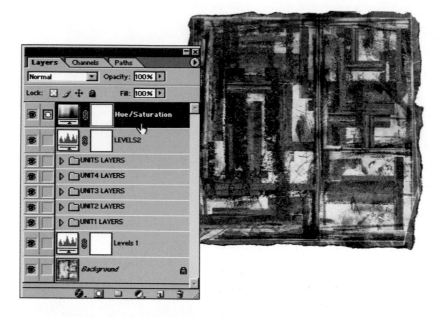

STEP 14

We can see that as a result of the last step, the brown color has been applied to the outline of the image as well. To keep this area white, click the Layer Mask Thumbnail icon to the left of the adjustment layer. Because we need a mask for the white areas, activate the Background layer at the very bottom of the Layers palette. Then use the Magic Wand tool from the Toolbox to select the white areas.

STEP 15

With the selection marquee active, return to the Hue/Saturation adjustment layer and click on the layer mask thumbnail to create a layer mask.

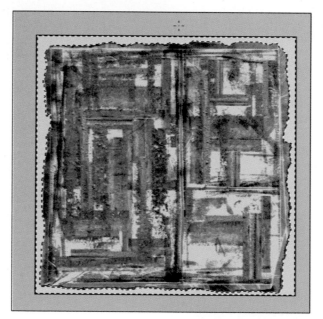

STEP 16

Set the background color to black in the Toolbox and fill the selection with black.

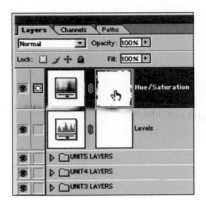

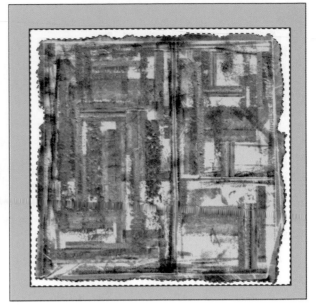

STEP 17

At this point, the basic background is complete. Now we will arrange the object files on top of this background. Before adding the "Body" image that will be used as our object, we need to reduce the number of layers so that our work is not slowed down. Adjust the Hue/Saturation settings on the adjustment layer again to adjust the brightness of the image. Click the triangular button located at the top right in the Layers palette and choose Flatten Image. (Caution: To be safe, save the file in native Photoshop format before applying the Flatten Image command. Then, save the file again with a different name after the Flatten command has been applied.)

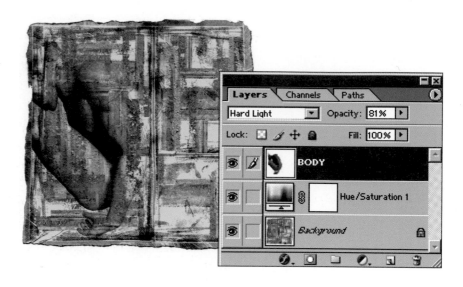

STEP 18

Copy and paste the "Body" image into the background image. Set the blending mode of the "Body" image to Hard Light at 80-100% so that it blends in with the background color.

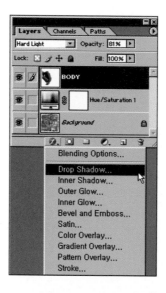

STEP 19

To add a lush shadow below the "Body" image, click on the Add a Layer Style button at the bottom left of the Layers palette and choose Drop Shadow.

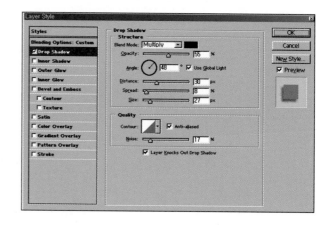

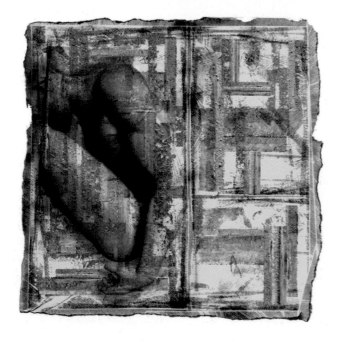

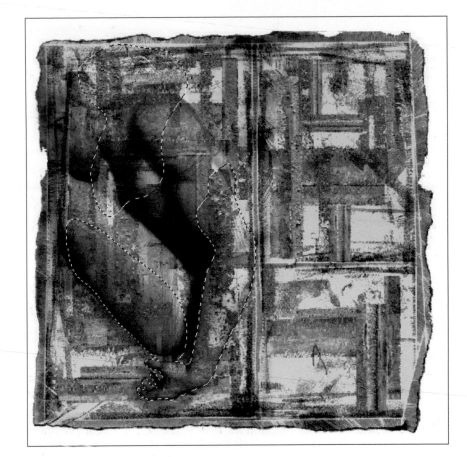

STEP 20

To emphasize the texture where the "Body" image overlaps the Background layer (shown here), use the Lasso tool or Path tool to select portions of both images and then copy and paste the blend. (We copied and pasted the head and the entire arms and legs of the "Body" image.)

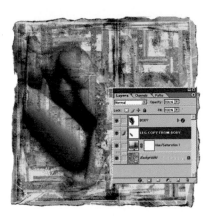

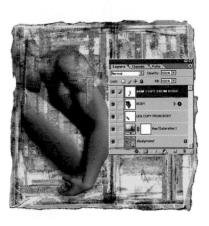

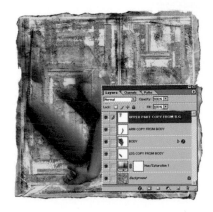

STEP 21

We set the duplicated images that were made into layers to the Overlay blending mode opacity of 60-80%. We can see that this strongly emphasizes the textures.

STEP 22

We need to cover up the holes that appear here and there in the image. We will repeat steps 8–9 to emphasize the textures while trying to cover up the empty spaces. First, copy and paste two or three unit images that were emphasized using steps 8–9 into the image. Adjust their sizes and give them different blending modes and opacities. (Because we are trying to cover up the holes as naturally as possible, we use lower opacity values than we did for the original background unit images.) Place these layers in a new layer set, named "Additional Units," and move the set below the Hue/Saturation adjustment layer so that all the units in the set will be the same color.

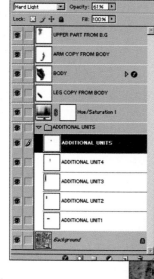

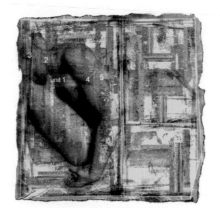

STEP 23

Blend the additional unit images as follows: 1 at Multiply mode at 64%, 2 at Multiply mode at 62%, 3 at Color Burn mode at 27%, 4 at Multiply mode at 40%, and 5 at Hard Light mode at 61%.

STEP 24

As we can see here, the "Body" image blends too well with the background. Therefore, we will darken the outline of the "Body" image so that it stands out. Simply darkening the outline carelessly will make the image seem unnatural. Instead, taking into account the outline pattern and direction of the background's unit images, we will use the Air Brush tool to paint. To do so, we first need to create a rough selection and remove (using the Subtract from Selection command) the outline of the "Body" image from the selection. Then, we create a new layer on which to paint. First, we will use the Lasso tool and click on the Background layer to activate it. Then, without paying attention to detail, we will select huge chunks of the background, as shown.

STEP 25

To create a roughened outline, apply steps 4-5 to alter the shape of the selection. The Tolerance value of the Magic Wand tool should be set to below 10 so that small selections can be made. Sticking with this will allow a very detailed outline to be created.

STEP 26

After the selections are made, press the [ctrl] and [alt] keys and click on the "Body" image layer to remove it from the selection marquee. (Mac users use the Command and Option keys.)

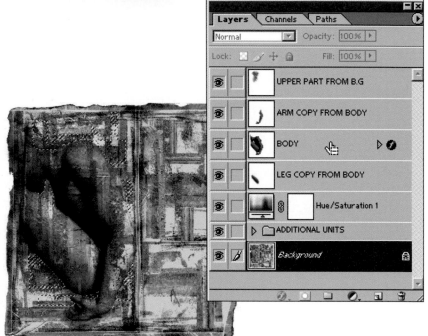

STEP 27

With the Background layer active, copy and paste to create a temporary layer for darkening the "Body" image. Naming this temporary layer "AroundBody," set its blending mode to Soft Light and the opacity value to 100%. (This blending mode is chosen because it allows us to darken or lighten colors.) Next we'll paint, using the Air Brush tool, in a dark brown color so that the area around the "Body" image is emphasized.

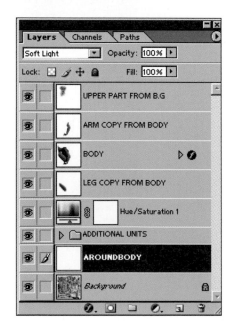

STEP 28

After choosing the Air Brush tool from the Toolbox, set the painting blending mode to Hard Light to create a dark color with a high contrast. Then, after setting the foreground color to a dark brown, we paint over the layer.

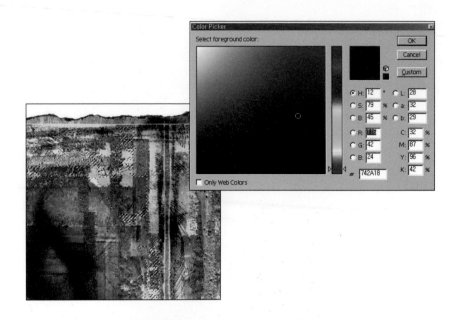

STEP 29

To further understand what we are doing here, the "AroundBody" layer is shown here at Normal mode and 100%. Now, we change it back to the original state.

STEP 30

The area around the "Body" image is completed (right). As shown in the preview of the completed image, metallic UFO images will be arranged in the image to create the effect of dimension. First, apply the Flatten Layer command to the previous layers.

STEP 31

Now open the "UFO" image, which we modeled and retouched using Corel Bryce®.

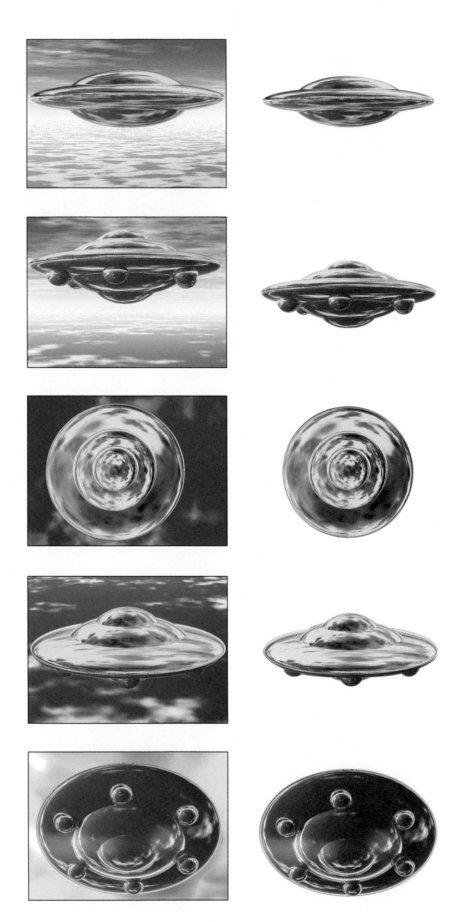

STEP 32

Because the image of the UFO appears too green compared to the entire image, lower the contrast so that it appears metallic. This is done simply by applying Hue/Saturation ([ctrl]+[u]) to each image.

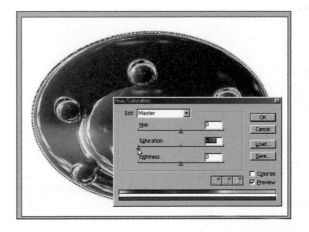

STEP 33

Adjusting the Hue/Saturation will also alter the brightness and contrast. Therefore, we choose Image > Adjust > Levels to add some contrast.

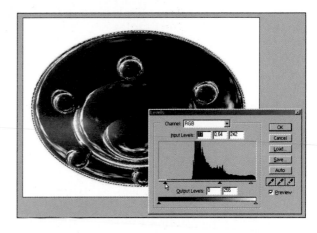

STEP 34

Now copy and paste the "UFO" images into the background image and arrange them using Free Transform ([ctrl]+[t]) to adjust their size and positions. When they are all in place, merge the five "UFO" layers into one layer by clicking the link icon next to each layer name in the Layers palette and then choosing Merge Linked from the Layers palette menu. Maintain the new layer's default blending mode and opacity (Normal, 100%).

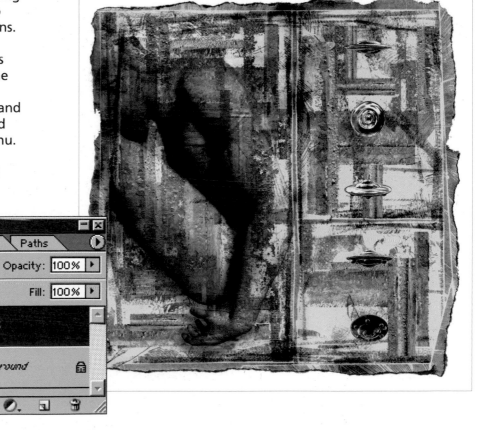

STEP 35

The preview of the completed image shows us that the UFOs must be placed within rectangular boxes and that shadows must be inserted around them. To do this, we use the Drop Shadow Layer effect. First, to create the box that will encompass the UFOs, create a new layer on top of the UFO layer. Then, use the Rectangular Marquee tool to draw a rectangle on top of each UFO. A fixed distance must be maintained between the rectangles when doing this. Using guides, create a rough framework for your selection based on the sizes of and distance between the images.

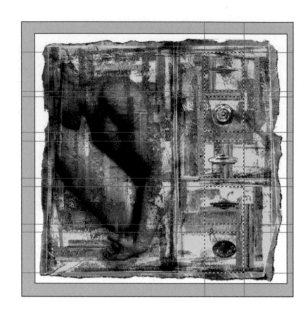

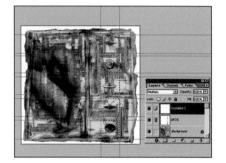

STEP 36

Next, choose Edit > Fill to fill in the rectangle in white and the layer is set to the Multiply mode at 100%. This will cause the white rectangle to disappear from the screen. (This rectangular layer is named "Squares.")

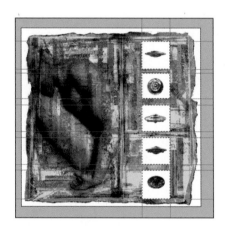

STEP 37

Choose Layer > Layer Style > Inner Shadow to add shadow to the inside of the rectangle. The Layer Style dialog box allows us to specify the color of the shadow. In keeping with the background, we will select a color as close to black as possible. Also, the Use Global Light next to the Angle field must not be selected because we want to use a different angle for each of the shadows.

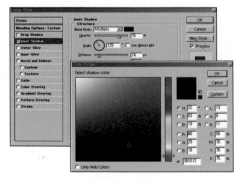

STEP 38

Next we will add shadows to the UFO images. After selecting a UFO image (click on a "UFO" layer while pressing the [ctrl] or Command keys), choose Drop Shadow from the Layer Style submenu and then adjust the size and direction of the shadow.

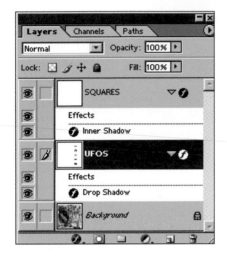

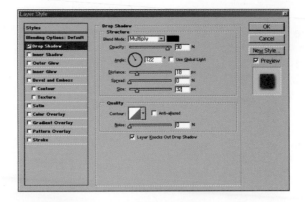

Project 5

Project 5 Source Files

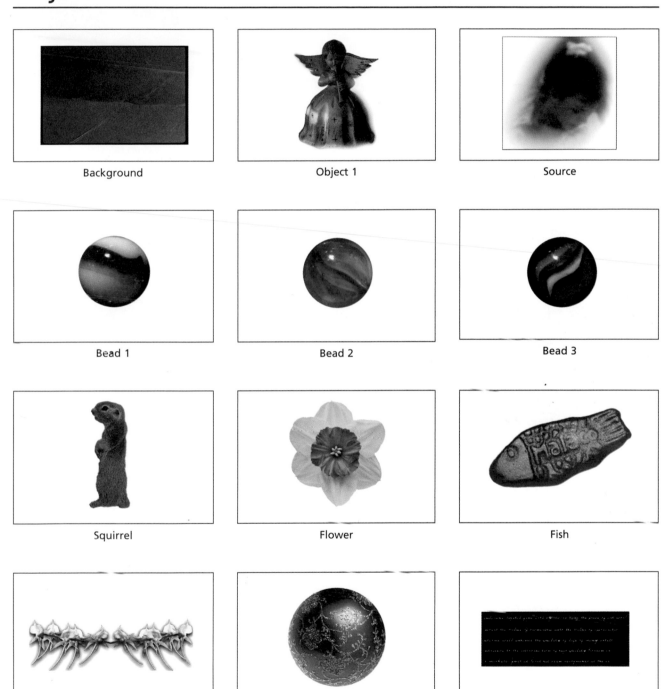

Background

Object 1

Source

Bead 1

Bead 2

Bead 3

Squirrel

Flower

Fish

Corolla

Water Drop

Text

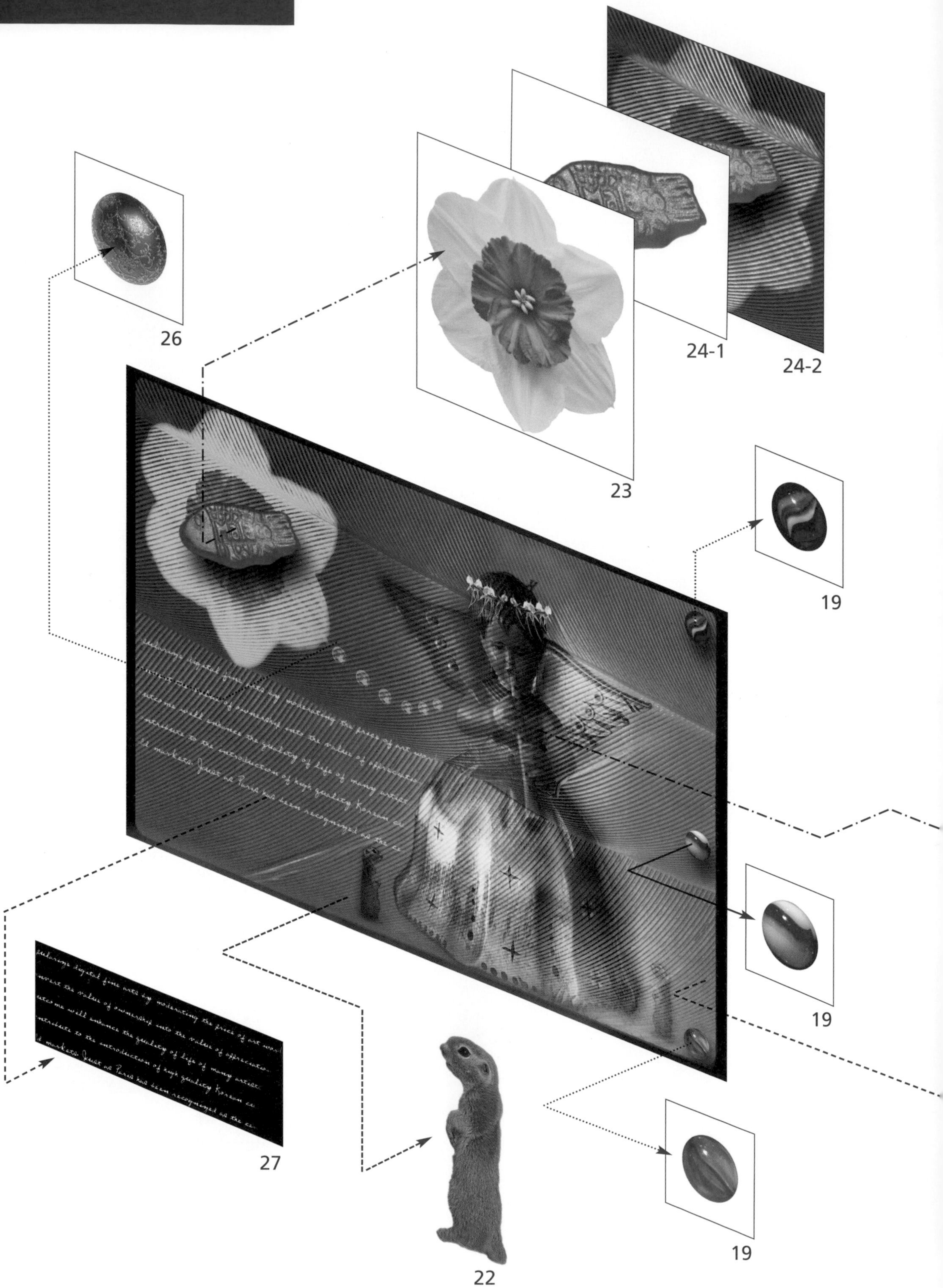

26

24-1

24-2

23

19

19

27

19

22

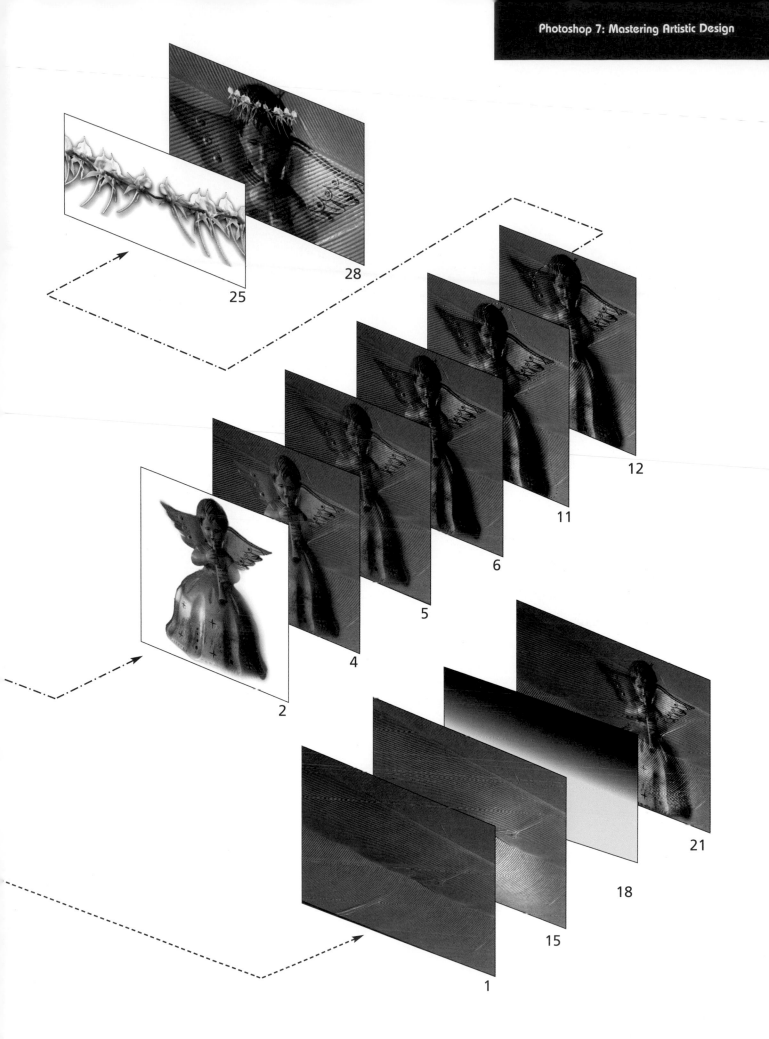

STEP 1

Open the "Background" texture file.

STEP 2

Open the "Object 1" image file. Select only the figure of the angel, without its background, and copy it. Activate the "Background" window again and paste the copied image. Name the new layer "Object 1."

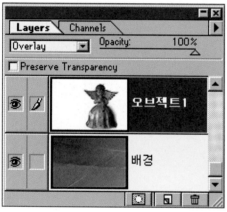

STEP 3

Set the blending mode of this layer to Overlay and leave the opacity at 100%.

STEP 4

Seen here is a comparison of the "Object 1" layer with and without the Overlay blending mode.

STEP 5

The Overlay blending mode creates the effect of having the background superimposed on top of the "Object 1" layer. To emphasize the background texture, first, make a copy of the "Object 1" layer. Name this new layer "Object 2." (Again, set the blending mode to Overlay and leave the opacity at 100%. This is done so that the sharpness, brightness, and hue of the "Object 1" layer harmonize with the background texture.) Directly adjusting the hue and brightness is another alternative. However, making a copy of the layer using the same blending mode is an effective way to emphasize hue and brightness variations and adds more depth to the final image.

STEP 6

To adjust the brightness of the "Object 1" layer, open the "Source file" image, select it (excluding the white background), and paste it into the composite image. You could use the Lasso tool or a path to make a selection and adjust the "Object 1" layer's brightness within that area. Instead, we'll use the "Source file" image to adjust the brightness of the "Object 1" image. You won't be able to see the "Source file" image itself, but it will help to create a natural finish.

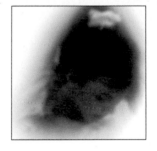

STEP 7

Name the new layer "Object Background" and set its blending mode to Exclusion and its opacity to 40%. This will lessen the abrupt brightness and hue variations between the background texture and the "Object 1" layer. Although no real difference can be seen with the naked eye, we are laying the groundwork for modifying the overall mood of the image. This must be kept in mind as we work through the steps on this page.

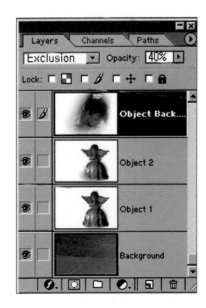

STEP 8

To darken the background of the "Object 1" layer, make a copy of the "Object Background" layer and adjust the blending mode to Difference and the opacity to 10%. Name this new layer "Object Background 2."

STEP 9

Step 8 creates a subtle shadow for the "Object 1" image. To select the area surrounding this image, click on the layer's name in the Layers palette while pressing the [ctrl] key. Use the Marquee tool to move this selection marquee and place it right about where the shadow for Object 1 should be.

STEP 10

Apply a Feather value of 50 to the selection.

STEP 11

Create another layer and name it "Shadow." (The selection will remain activated even when creating a new layer.)

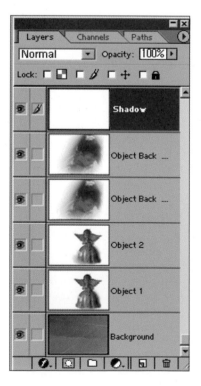

STEP 12

Place the "Object Background" and "Shadow" layers below "Object 1" and "Object 2" in the Layers palette. This is done to add shadow to the background of Object 1.

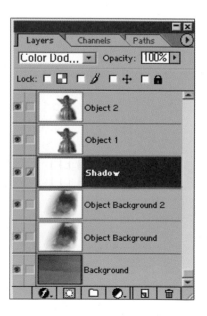

STEP 13

Set the foreground color to dark gray and choose Edit > Fill to fill the selection. Then set the blending mode to Color Dodge and the opacity to 100%. Although we filled in the selection with a dark color, the image appears lighter because the blending mode is set to Color Dodge. The image here shows only the blending of the "Shadow" layer with the background. All other layers have been hidden. We can see the difference from the original background image that we started with in Step 1.

STEP 14

Drop the selection and choose Layer > Add Layer Mask > Reveal All to create a mask for the "Shadow" layer.

STEP 15

Switch to the Gradient tool and choose the Black, White gradient. Apply a gradient to the layer mask as seen here.

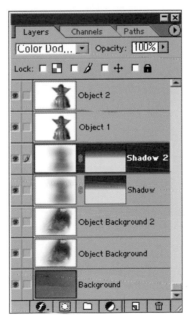

STEP 16

Now we'll make a copy of the "Shadow" layer in order to modify its hue and brightness. Name the duplicated layer "Shadow 2." Move the layer image to the area that will be modified. Then, press [ctrl] and click on the "Object 1" layer to create a selection of the area; press Delete to remove the portion of the shadow that falls within the selection. This is done not to change the overall color and hue of the "Object 1" layer, but to create a shadowed effect around it. Choose Layer > Remove Layer Mask > Apply to get rid of the mask on the "Shadow 2" layer.

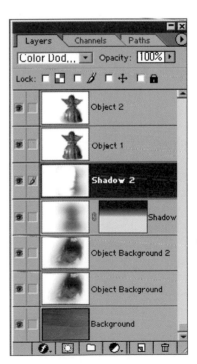

STEP 17

Repeat Step 16 to adjust the depth of the shadow incrementally. As more and more shadow layers are created, the shadow deepens to create a more naturalistic texture. We will end the discussion of texture here.

STEP 18

The image here shows the completion of the shadow work.

STEP 19

Open the next group of image files and select their contents (without their respective backgrounds), paste the images into the composite, and name the new layers "Bead 1," "Bead 2," and "Bead 3." Retain the default blending mode and opacity settings for these new layers (Normal, 100%).

STEP 20

Click on the topmost bead layer and choose Layer > Merge Down to combine the three layers into one. Then situate the marbles as shown.

STEP 21

Now we will create a shadow for each marble. Choose Layer > Layer Style > Drop Shadow or click the Add a Layer Style button at the bottom of the Layers palette and choose Drop Shadow. Make your preferred settings for the size, color, and location of the shadows for the beads.

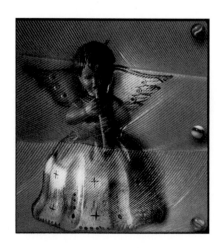

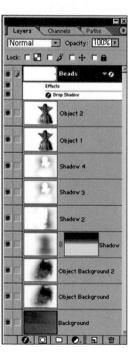

STEP 22

Open the "Squirrel" image file, select the squirrel, and drag it into the composite image. Name the new layer "Squirrel" and set its blending mode to Overlay, leaving its opacity to 100%. Adjust the size of the layer and situate it in the desired position. Make a copy of this layer and flip it vertically to create another squirrel on the other side of the angel. Again, once the images have been placed in the desired positions, merge the layers into one.

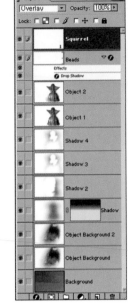

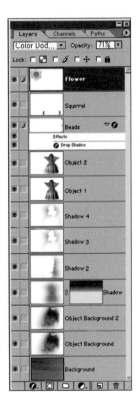

STEP 23

Open the "Flower" image. Select the flower and drag it into the composite image. Name the new layer "Flower" and set its blending mode to Color Dodge and its opacity to 70%. Then position it on the background as shown here.

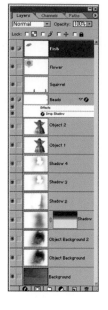

STEP 24

Next, open the "Fish" image, select the fish, and drag it into the composite image. Name the new layer "Fish" and leave its blending mode set to Normal and its opacity at 100%. Give the "Fish" layer a drop shadow by choosing Layer > Layer Style > Drop Shadow or by clicking the Add a Layer Style button at the bottom of the Layers palette and choosing Drop Shadow.

STEP 25

Open the "Corolla" image. This image is the ornamental crown that will be placed on the head of the angel. Select the crown and drag it into the composite image. Name the new layer "Corolla" and leave its blending mode set at Normal and its opacity at 100%.

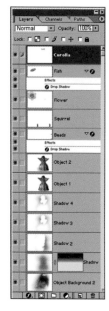

STEP 26

Open the "Water Drop" image, select its contents, and drag them into the composite image. Name the resulting layer "Water Drop." Set its blending mode to Color Dodge and its opacity to 85%. The "Water Drop" image will be used to link the angel with the flower. Make several copies of the "Water Drop" layer and then resize and position the droplets using Free Transform. Combine the "Water Drop" layers, from the top down, into one layer with the Merge Down command.

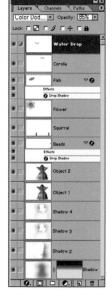

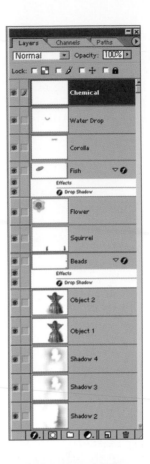

STEP 27

Finally, open the "Text" image. Copy the image and paste it into a new channel in the composite image. Press the [ctrl] key as you click on the channel in the Channels palette to create a selection from it. Create a new layer and choose Edit > Fill to fill the selection with white.

Project 6

Project 6 Source Files

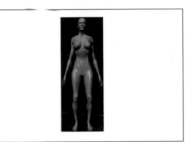

Background

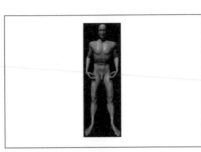

Man

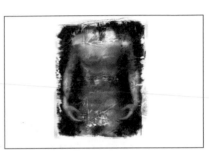

Man Distressed

Woman

Woman Distressed

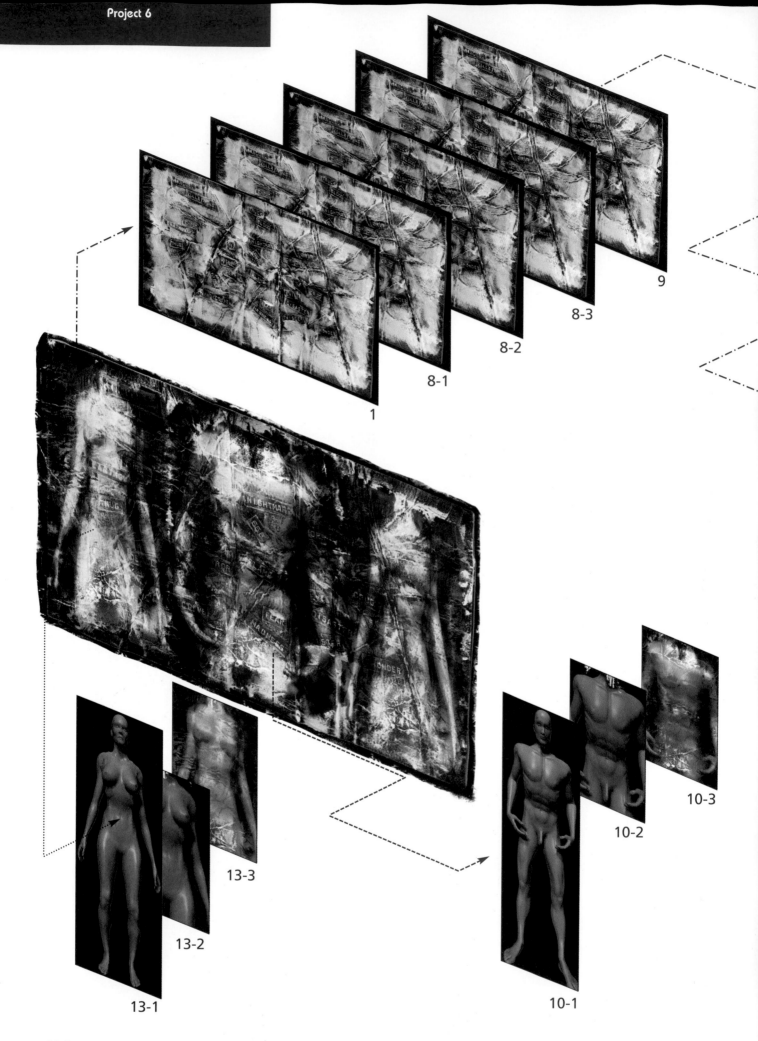

8-1

8-2

8-3

9

1

13-3

13-2

13-1

10-1

10-2

10-3

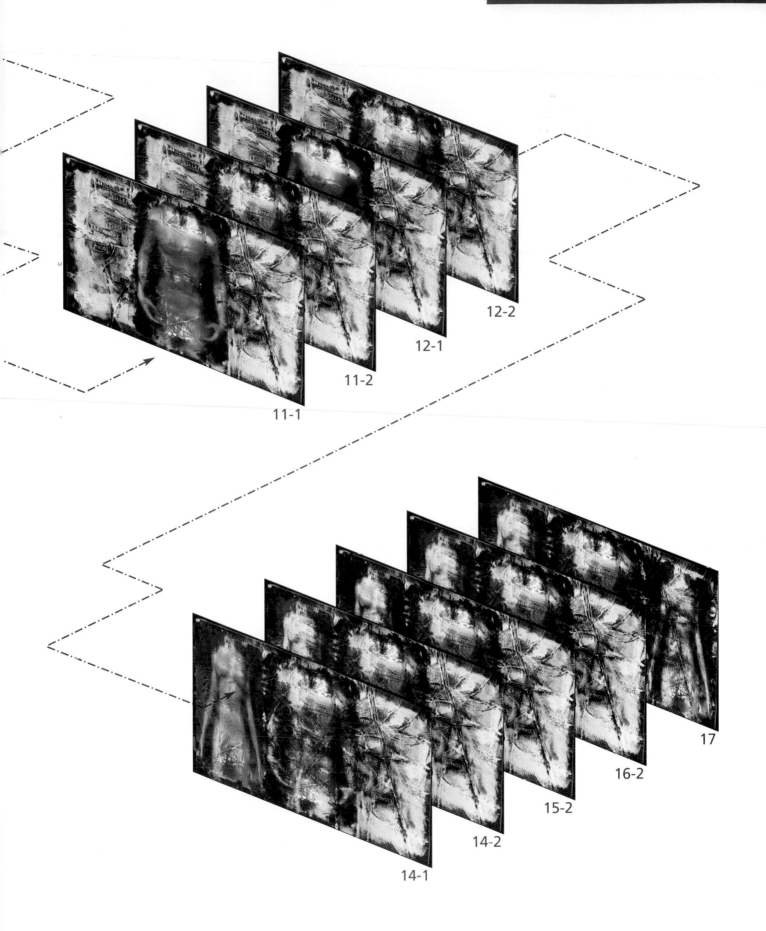

11-1

11-2

12-1

12-2

14-1

14-2

15-2

16-2

17

STEP 1

Open the scanned "Background" image that will be used as the background.

STEP 2

Before we start working with this image, zoom in on some areas within it so we can go over the way it was created (without regard to the order in which it was done). To make this image, we created labels using a handheld label maker and used them to create a collage on thick black paper.

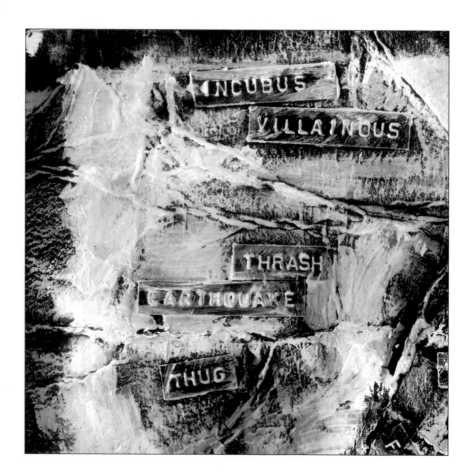

STEP 3

The text of the labels deals with the emotion of fear.

STEP 4

The thick black paper was slightly crumpled and modeling paste was painted over it to enhance its texture.

STEP 5

The outer edges of the background were painted slightly
lighter and the outer edges
were left black to create a
frame for the image.

STEP 6

To emphasize the crumpled
texture of the paper, a blade
was used to create deep random scratches.

STEP 7

The background thus created was scanned in grayscale mode; now we'll add some color to it. First, convert the image to RGB mode. (This image was created using the RGB mode.) Make a copy of the Background layer and name it "Background." Make sure this layer's blending mode is Normal and its opacity is 100%.

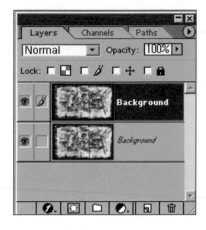

STEP 8

To create a faded texture, change the image's color to a brownish tone. Choose Image > Adjustment > Color Balance and adjust the values for the Highlights, Midtones, and Shadows (each in turn, without leaving the dialog box) as shown here and on the next page. Creating this color is a very important step in the overall process, so we will go over the contents of the Color Balance dialog box in some detail.

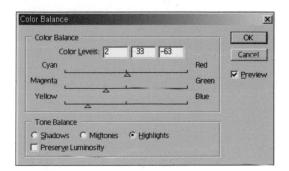

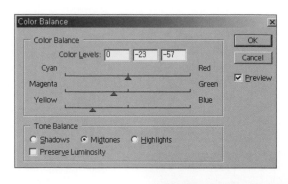

STEP 9

After the Color Balance command is used to add color, adjust the image's brightness and contrast.

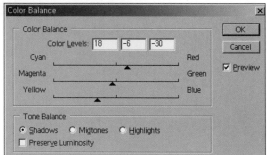

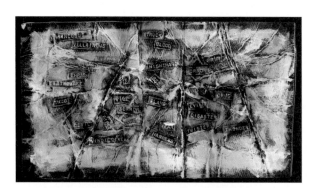

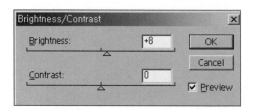

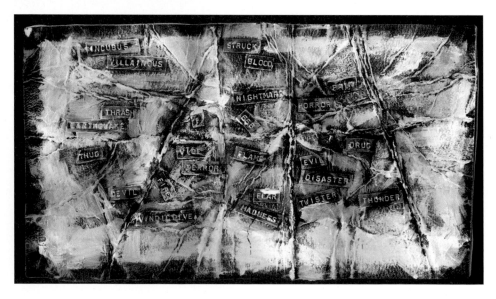

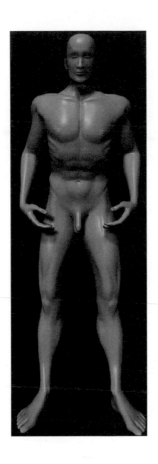

STEP 10

You can use the "Man" file and distress it yourself, or you can use the "Man Distressed" file that we provide. Open the image file and use the Move tool to drag its contents into the composite image. This image was rendered using Curious Labs Poser® program and retouched using Procreate Painter®. For further details, refer to "Working with Other Graphic Tools" in the back of this book.

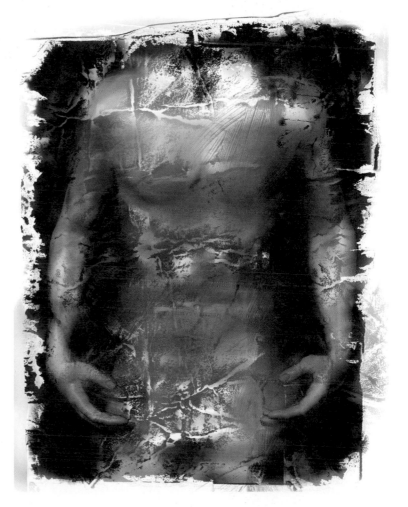

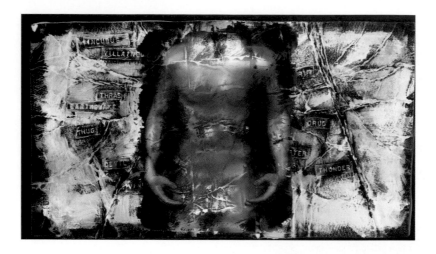

STEP 11

Name the new layer "Man" and set its blending mode to Hard Light and its opacity to 100%. Then, center the image on the background. The following images are experiments with different blending modes.

STEP 12

As we can see here, the background texture of the "Man" layer is very powerful. To offset that, we'll add some soft noise. Duplicate the "Man" layer and name it "Man 2." Place "Man 2" below "Man" in the Layers palette. Set the blending mode to Dissolve and the opacity to 9%. This creates a slightly roughened image with subtle noise. Keeping the blending mode the same but changing the opacity to 100% reduces the overall texture of the background and creates more noise. Below is a comparison of the images at both opacities.

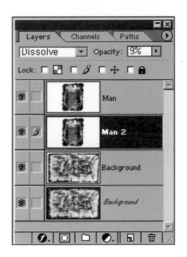

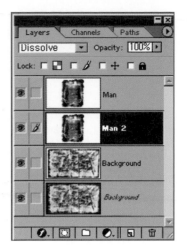

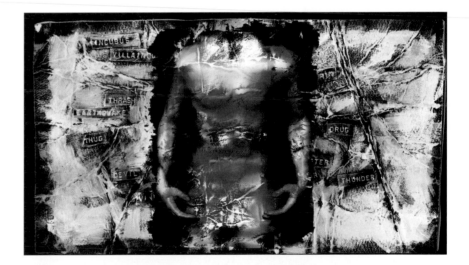

STEP 13

Now we'll add the image of a woman. You can use the "Woman" image file and distress it yourself or use the version we supply, "Woman Distressed." Open the image file, select the image (excluding the white background), and use the Move tool to drag the selection into the composite image and place it to the left of the "Man" image.

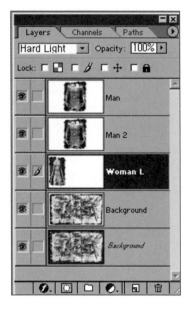

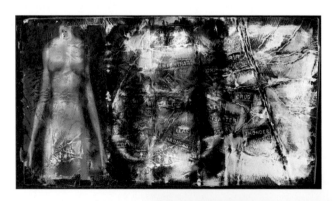

STEP 14

Name the new layer "Woman L" and set its blending mode to Hard Light and its opacity to 100%. Place this layer below both the "Man" and "Man 2" layers. Following is a comparison of the image using different blending modes for the "Woman L" layer.

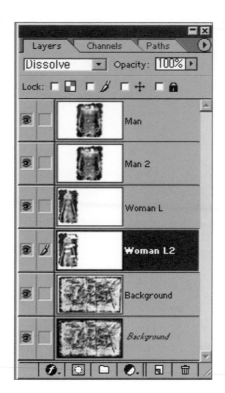
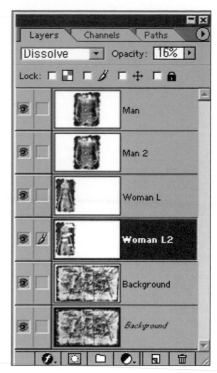

STEP 15

Follow the same procedure used for the "Man" layer: To add noise, duplicate the "Woman L" layer and name it "Woman L2." Then place this duplicated layer below the original layer in the Layers palette. Set the blending mode to Dissolve and the opacity to 16%. Following is a comparison of the image at different opacities.

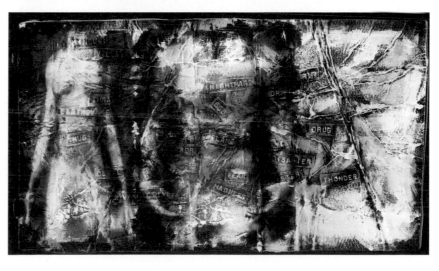

STEP 16

To create the image of a woman for the right side of the man, simply make one copy each of the "Woman L" and "Woman L2" layers and place them to the right of the "Man" layer. To add some variety, we will slightly modify the image of the woman on the right. Because the background texture behind "Woman L" is different from the background texture behind "Woman R," two images already have some individuality. However, to give some variety to the images themselves, we will modify the opacity values. Using the same blending mode (Dissolve), set the opacity value of "Woman R2" to 12%.

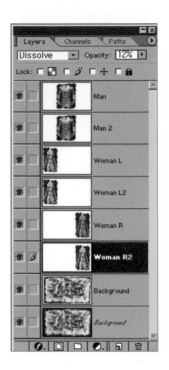

STEP 17

Here we have magnified portions of the completed image. We do this to see the detailed blending of the images with the background.

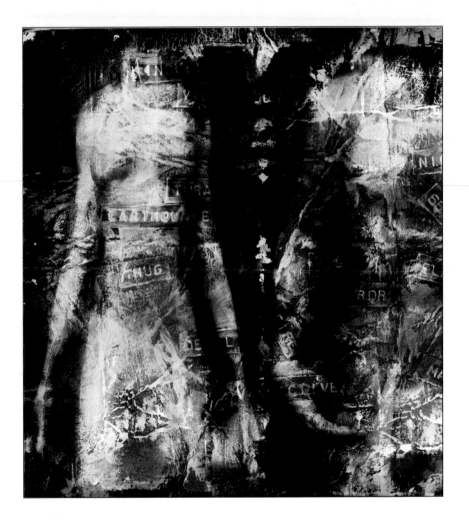

STEP 18
We used Procreate Painter® to
add edge detail and texture to
complete the image.

Project 7

Project 7 Source Files

Painting

Face 1

Face 2

Face 3

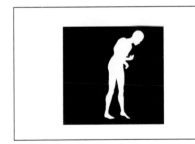

Object 1

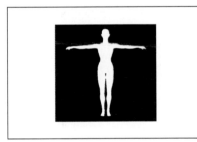

Object 2

Object 3

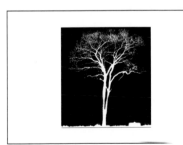

Object 4

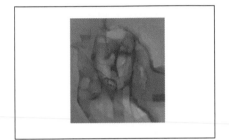

Tree

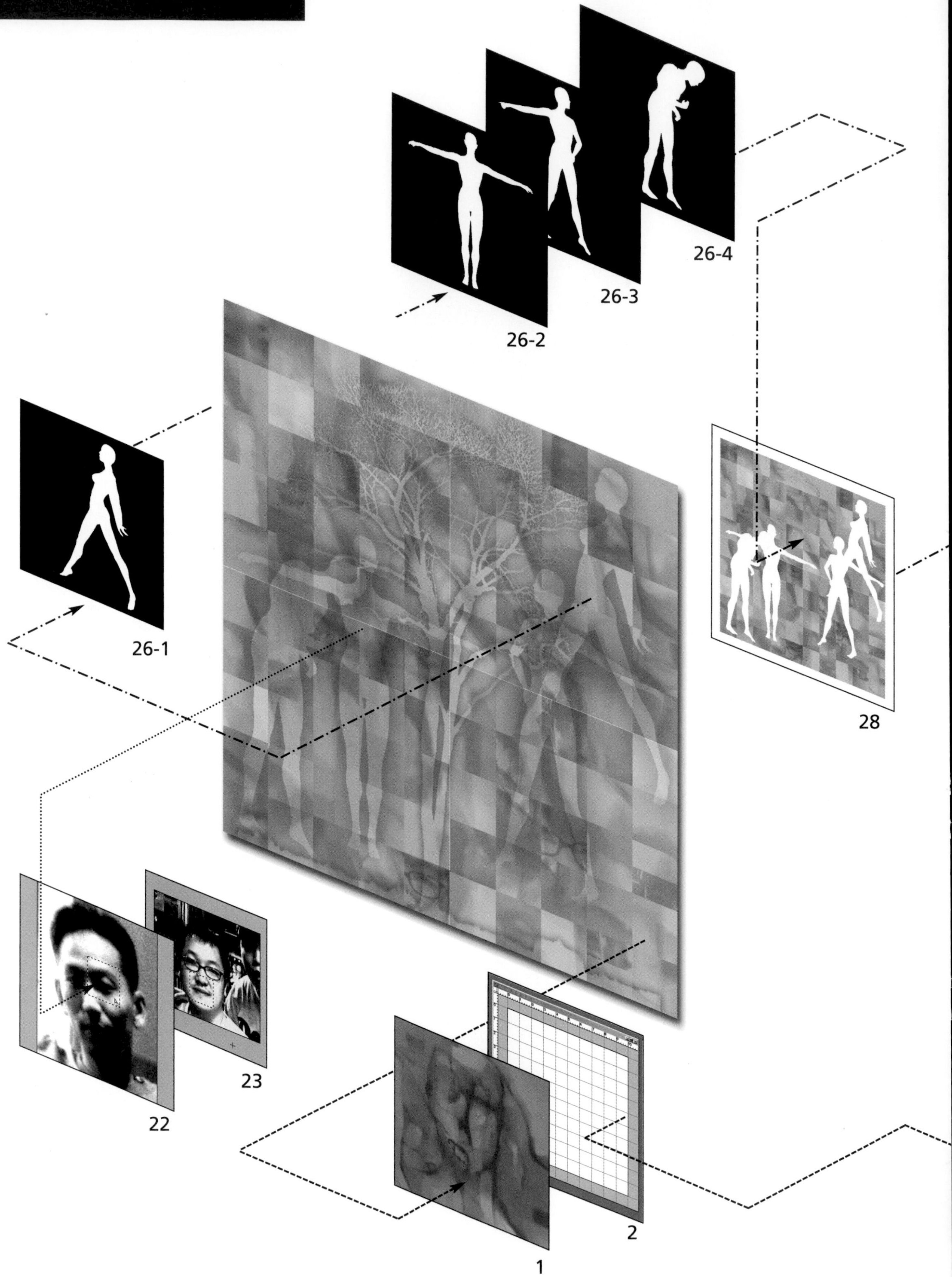

26-1

26-2

26-3

26-4

28

22

23

1

2

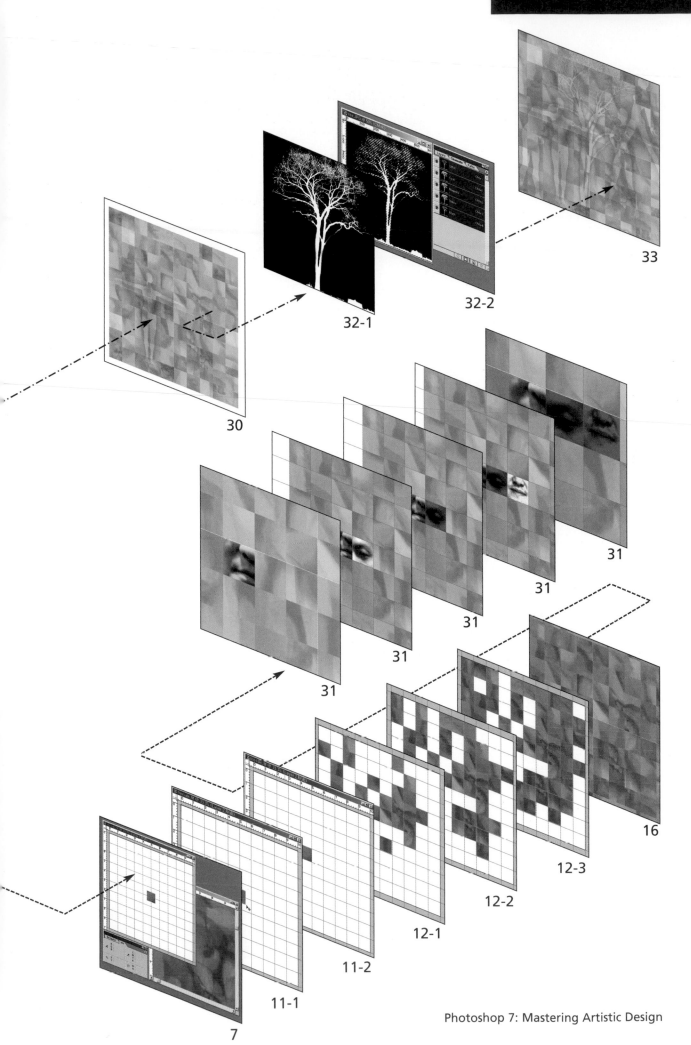

33

32-1

32-2

30

31

31

31

31

31

31

16

12-3

12-2

12-1

11-2

11-1

7

Introduction

Project 7 focuses on creating one image as a mosaic and then using it as a background for another project. Mosaic work entails using the simplest techniques to create maximum results. There is no need to add detail and realism to mosaic images because the images will be used to create one complex background. The ease with which the tools can be used in this project is one of its greatest advantages. The complex background that was shown earlier can be created by merely using the Marquee tool, the Move tool, and guides.

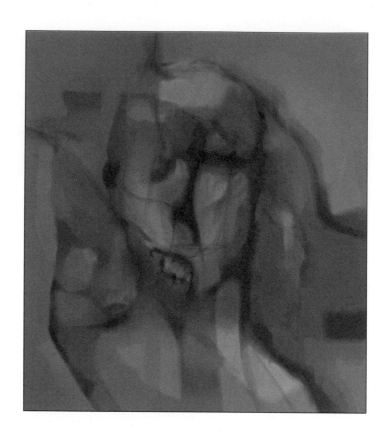

STEP 1

Open the "Painting" image file.

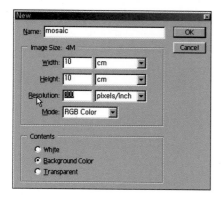

STEP 2

Press [ctrl]+[n] (or Command+[n]) to create a new document in which the mosaic background will be made. The important thing to remember here is that the Resolution values for the source image and the new document should be the same. We will call this new document "Mosaic."

STEP 3

Next, we put guides into place for a more accurate mosaic. These guides are necessary to place the rectangles, which must be all the same size. Press [ctrl]+[r] or Command+[r] to show the rulers.

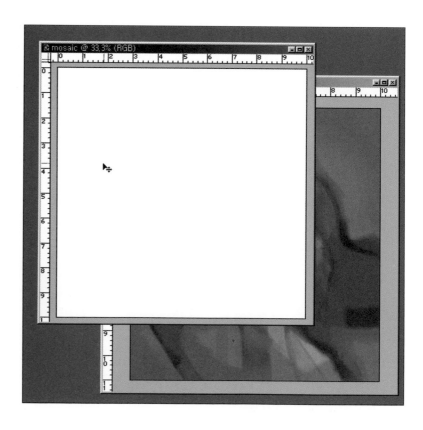

STEP 4

Place the cursor over the ruler and then drag the mouse. It does not matter which tool in the Toolbox is selected. Drag the mouse to create horizontal and vertical guides, 1 cm apart, on the page. Pay close attention to the X,Y positions on top of the guides in the Information palette.

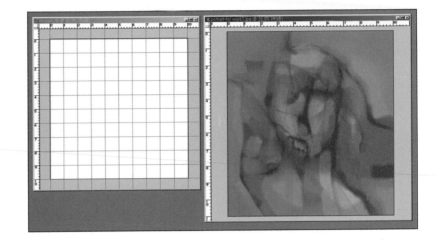

STEP 5

Draw a precise grid with 10 boxes each, vertically and horizontally. This will require 11 guidelines vertically and horizontally. We should have a total of 100 boxes in the grid. This brings us to the end of the preparations needed to create the mosaic.

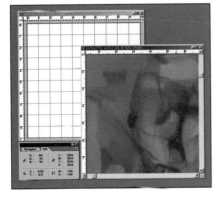

STEP 6

Click the source image window to activate it and use the Marquee tool to create a 1 cm rectangular selection in a random location somewhere on the page. Press the [shift] key while dragging and check the Info palette to create a selection frame that is exactly 1 cm square.

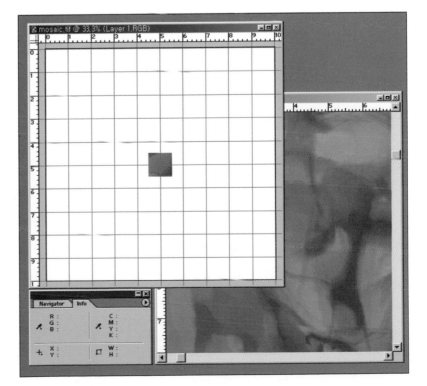

STEP 7

Press [ctrl]+[c] to copy the selected area. Then, click on the "Mosaic" window to activate it and press [ctrl]+[v] (or Command+[v]) to paste the copied selection.

STEP 8

The copied portion of the source image should be aligned with the grid for the time being. In order to do this, choose View > Snap and choose both the Guides and Document Bounds options.

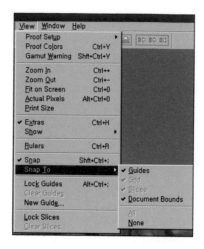

STEP 9

Use the Move tool to arrange the copied image in the desired location.

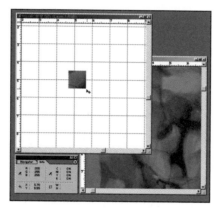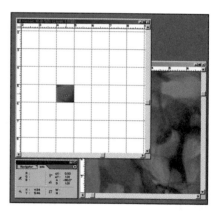

STEP 10

Now we'll add the second square to the mosaic. Click the source image window to activate it. Because the active selection marquee is already 1 cm square, you don't need to create a new selection; just move the selection marquee to another area of the image and copy that area.

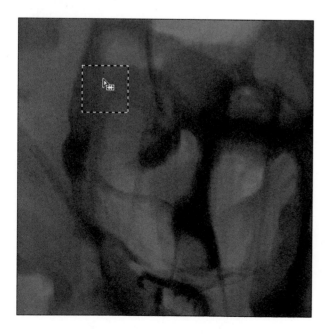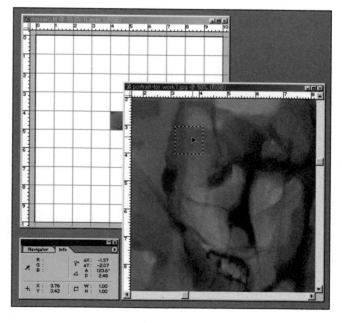

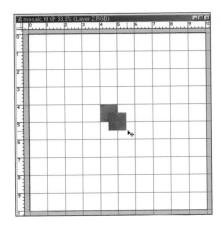
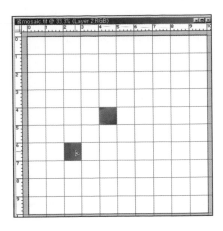

STEP 11

Repeat step 10 to arrange the image pasted into "Mosaic" in the desired position.

STEP 12

Repeat the steps above to fill in the empty squares one at a time. Of course, at any time, should the results be unsatisfactory, the positions can be changed or another portion of the source image can be copied and pasted. Continue to repeat these steps until a natural-looking result is attained.

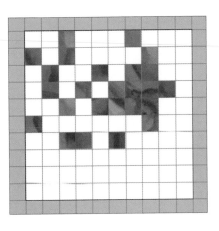

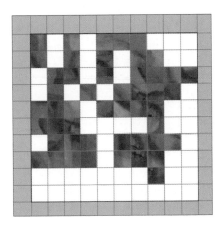

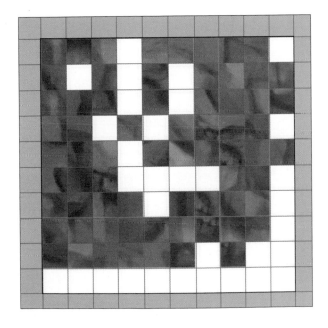

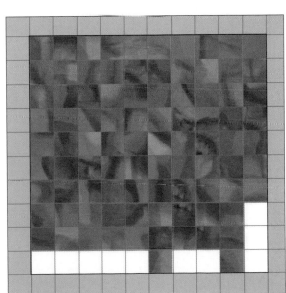

STEP 13

Use the Hide command
([ctrl]+[h] or Command+[h]) to
temporarily hide the guides
and view the images that have
been filled in so far. From this
point on, the Hide command
should be used frequently to
verify the results while working. This, of course, is because
the guides are distracting
when viewing the image.

STEP 14

If a portion of the mosaic sticks out, or if you do not like the
position of one of the arranged boxes, or if you want to change
the direction of a square, these kinds of modifications can be
made at any time. To change the direction of a square, first activate its layer and then use the Free Transform command
([ctrl]+[t] or Command+[t]). Drag outside the bounding border
to rotate the image and drag a handle to adjust the size.
Continue doing this until the image is satisfactory.

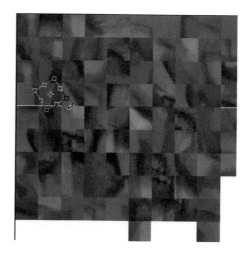

STEP 15

After you've pasted in more
than 100 square images, it
becomes quite tricky to select
the desired layer. In these
instances, select the Move tool
from the toolbar and then
[ctrl]+click on the desired square.
This makes it easy to select the
layer of a particular square.

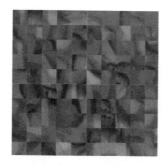

STEP 16

The completed mosaic image
appears slightly dark. To give it
an overall pastel tone, choose
Image > Adjust > Levels.

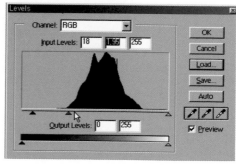

STEP 17

As we saw in the preview of the completed work earlier in this chapter, the image is surrounded by a white area, serving as a background for a soft drop shadow that adds a realistic touch to the image. To make this white border, set the background color to white in the Toolbox and then choose Image > Canvas Size to increase the image's vertical and horizontal area.

STEP 18

The background is, for the most part, complete. All we need to do now is to add some embellishment to portions of it. Open the three portraits that are needed for this process.

STEP 19

Again, we use steps 1-13 to copy portions of these portraits into the mosaic image. This is so that traces of a face are visible in parts of the background. After clicking on the desired image window to activate it, use the Rectangular Marquee tool to draw a 1 cm selection frame.

STEP 20

After copying, paste the square into the mosaic. Because of the Snap feature, the image can be precisely situated.

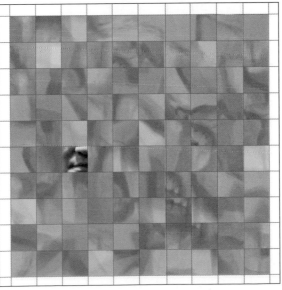

STEP 21

The pasted image is a black and white image. We will change the color to give it a brownish tone. Press [ctrl]+[u] or Command+[u] and then enter the values shown in the Hue/Saturation dialog box. Check the Colorize option. The color of the image has now been transformed to a dark brown tone.

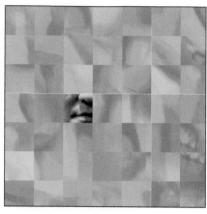

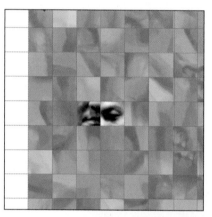

STEP 22

Click in the second window to activate it and, as shown, select and copy an area of it and arrange it in the desired location. Then, press [ctrl]+[u] or Command+[u] to apply the Hue/Saturation command to give the image a dark brown tone.

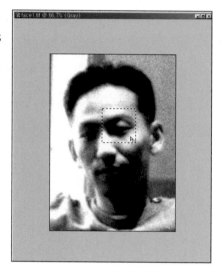

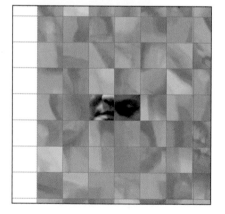

STEP 23

Select an area in the third image and repeat the steps above.

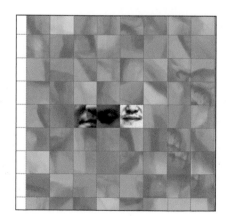

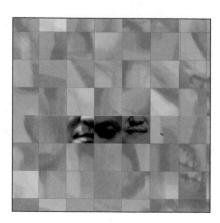

STEP 24

Set the blending mode of all three new layers to Multiply. This causes a slight smearing of the background texture over the face images.

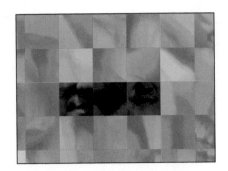
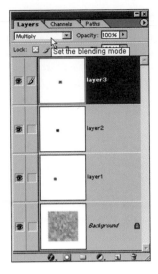

STEP 25

Because our objective was to create an image with an overall pastel tone, we set the opacity of the layers of each of the three portraits to 30%. The portraits should now be vaguely visible in the background.

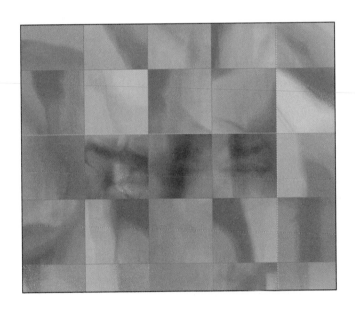

STEP 26

Repeating the steps above, copy more portions of the three portraits and arrange them in several places in the mosaic. The background is now complete.

STEP 27

We will now add a small number of objects to this background to complete the entire picture. These images were created using Poser 4® from Curious Labs®.

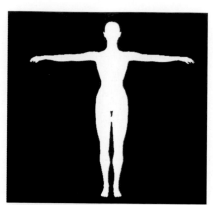

STEP 28

Open the four model images and open the Channels palette. [ctrl]+click on a random color channel in this palette and then select the white areas in the image. Drag and drop the white areas of the model image onto the mosaic image.

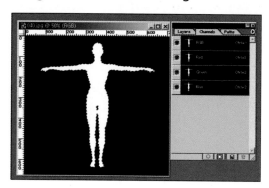

STEP 29

Repeat the step above for the three remaining model images and arrange them roughly on the mosaic background.

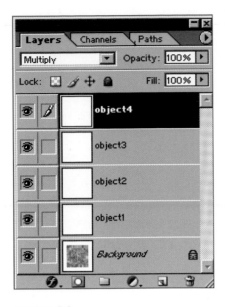

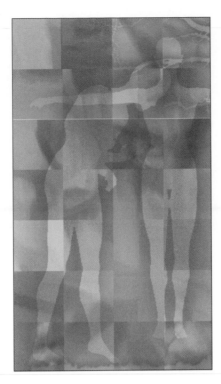

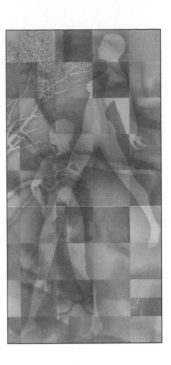

STEP 30

Referring back to the preview of the completed image, we see that the interiors of the objects are transparent, allowing the background to show through, and that there is a slight smear of shadow around the edges of these objects. To create a transparent interior, first set the blending mode of all the object layers to Multiply. This should make the objects disappear from the window.

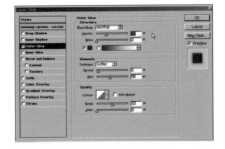

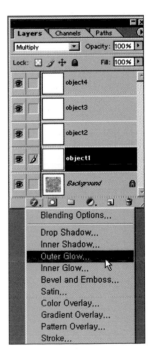

STEP 31

Now, use a layer style to add a dark glow to the edges of the objects. Let's first activate one object layer. Click the Add Layer Style button in the Layers palette and choose Outer Glow. The effect shown here should be seen.

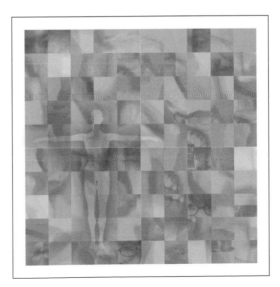

STEP 32

Apply this glow effect to the remaining object layers. The value of the Outer Glow should be the same for all the layers.

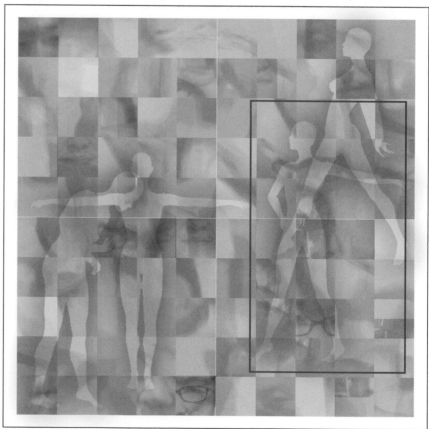

STEP 33

Open the final object, the "Tree" image. [ctrl]+click a random color channel in the Channel palette and then select the white areas of the image. Drag and load the white areas onto the mosaic and then apply an Outer Glow layer style to create a shadow.

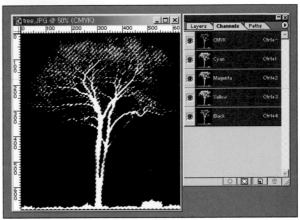

STEP 34

Again, set the blending mode of the "Tree" layer to Multiply. Using the Free Transform command, press [ctrl]+[t] to magnify the image of the tree and center it on the mosaic.

STEP 35

Now we'll merge all the layers into one. Choose Flatten Image from the Layers palette menu. Then show the hidden guides by choosing View > Show > Guides.

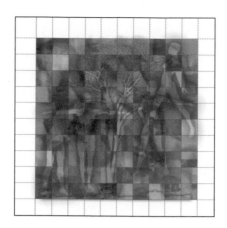

STEP 36

To add a soft shadow to the rectangular image, use the Rectangular Marquee tool to select the entire image, excluding the white frame. Because of the Snap feature, the square selection should be easy to create without having to press the [shift] key.

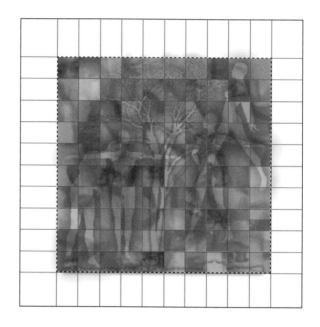

STEP 37

Because a layer style cannot be applied to the Background layer, duplicate the Background layer. Then, click the eye icon to temporarily hide the Background layer.

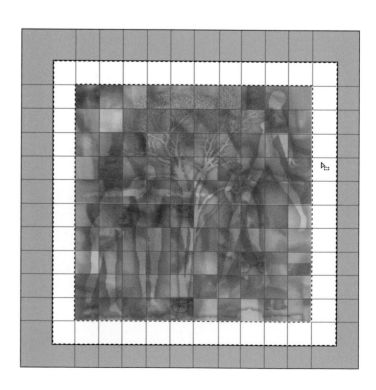

STEP 38

Choose Select > Inverse and press the [shift] key so that the white frame is removed from the layer. Now a shadow can be applied.

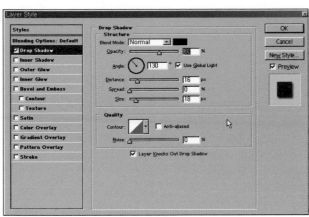

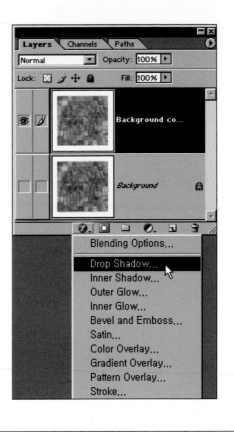

STEP 39

Clicking the Add Layer Style button, choose Drop Shadow and enter the values shown to add the shadow effect and complete the work.

Photoshop 7: Mastering Artistic Design

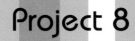

Project 8

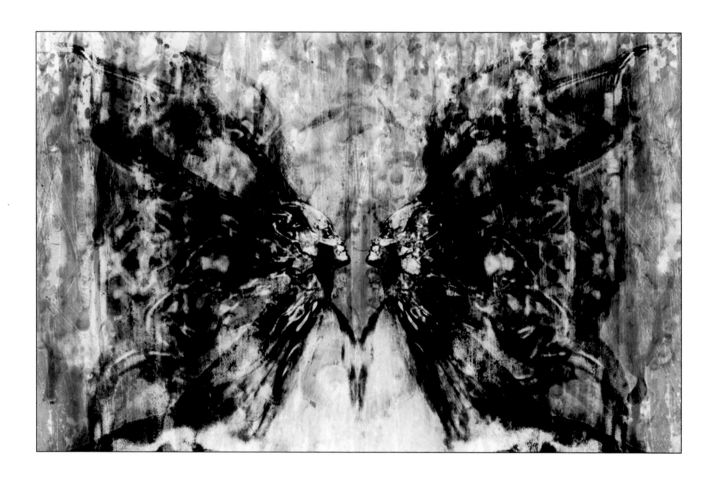

Project 8 Source Files

Picture

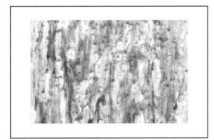

Background 01

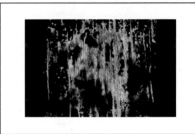

Background 02

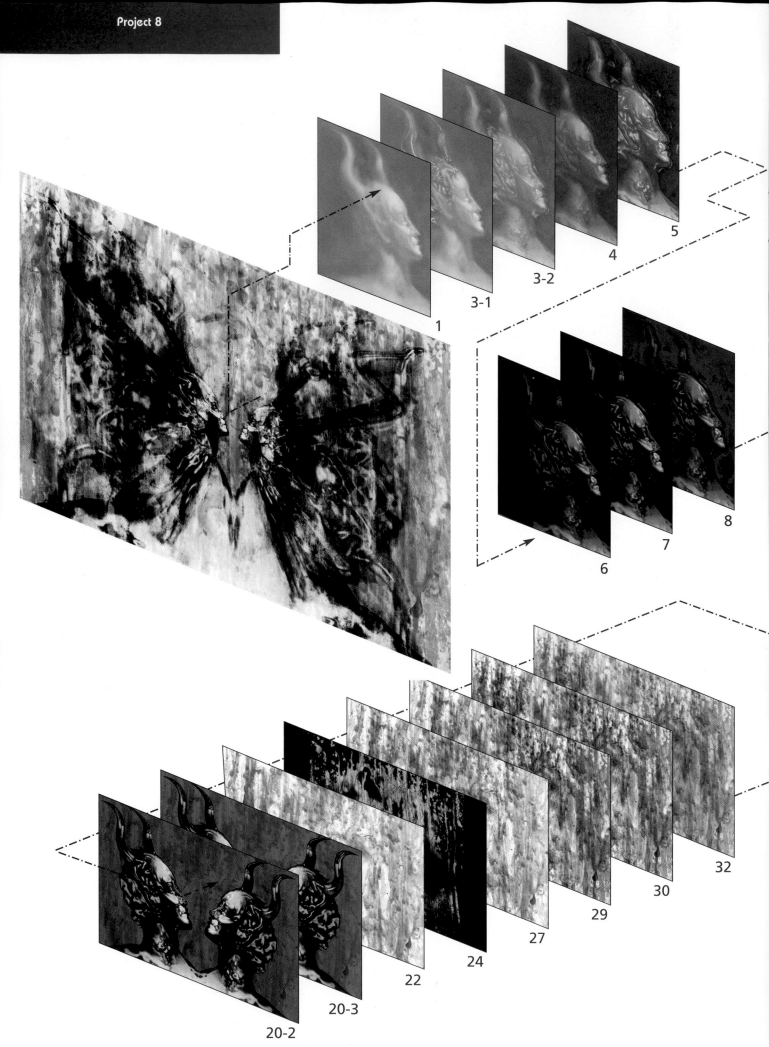

1

3-1

3-2

4

5

6

7

8

20-2

20-3

22

24

27

29

30

32

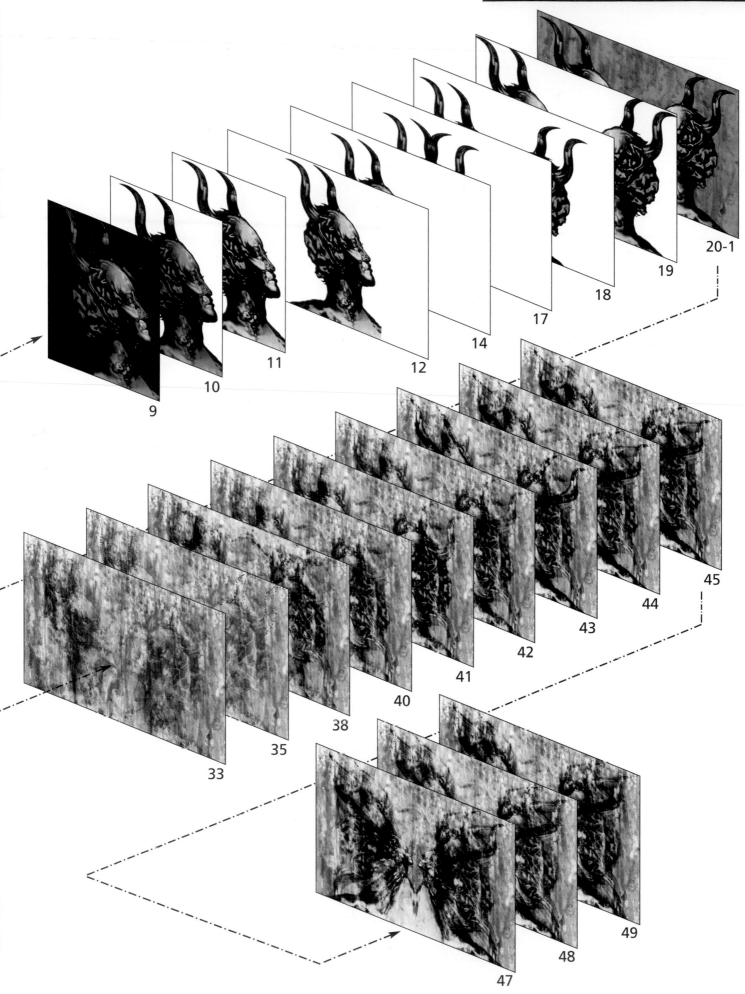

9

10

11

12

14

17

18

19

20-1

33

35

38

40

41

42

43

44

45

47

48

49

STEP 1

Open the "Picture" image. (This file was created using the Brush tool in Procreate Painter®.)

STEP 2

We are going to add some dimension to this flat image. Open the Layers palette and duplicate the "Background" layer. (Drag and drop the layer on the Create New Layer button located at the bottom of the Layers palette.) Name the new layer "Drawing." The blending mode will be adjusted after dimension is added. Choose Filter > Artistic > Plastic Wrap and adjust the Highlight Strength, Detail, and Smoothness settings. Although these values can be adjusted differently for different portions of the image, it works better for this image to modify the entire image at once. (If, after applying this filter, you want to work more on some portions of the image, select the areas in question using the Lasso tool and feather the selection before applying the Plastic Wrap filter.)

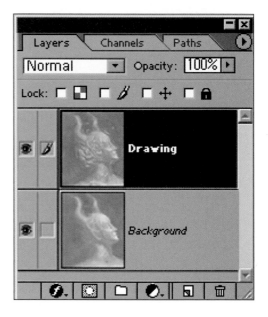

STEP 3

These two images show the difference between applying the Plastic Wrap filter to the entire image and to portions of the image.

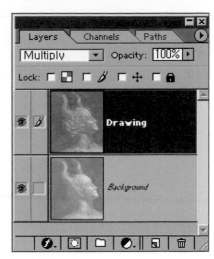

STEP 4

After applying the filter, set the layer's blending mode to Multiply and its opacity to 100%.

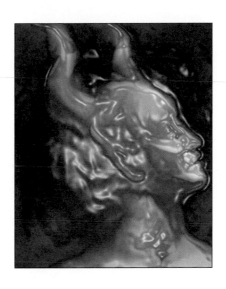

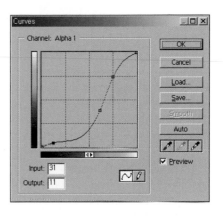

STEP 5

Adjust the curve for the "Drawing" layer as shown here. A variety of different effects can be obtained by modifying the curve.

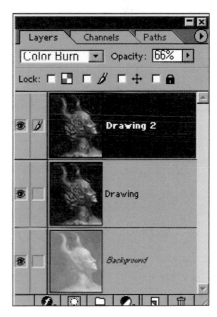

STEP 6

After adjusting the Curves, make another copy of this layer and call it "Drawing 2." Then set the blending mode to Color Burn and the opacity to 60%.

STEP 7

Adjust the curve for "Drawing 2" as shown to the right.

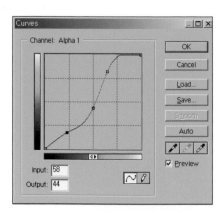

STEP 8

Try experimenting with the Curves option for other layers for a variety of different effects. The image above is just one example.

STEP 9

Combine all the layers into one "Background" layer by choosing Layer > Flatten Image.

STEP 10

Use the Lasso tool to select the head. Then open the Channels palette and create a new channel to save the selection by clicking the Save Selection as Channel button. Return to the "Background" layer. (Remember, all previous layers have been condensed into this one layer.) Set the background color to white in the Toolbox. Invert the selection frame, which is still active, and press the [del] key to remove the black area around the head.

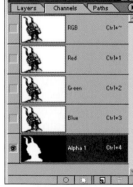

STEP 11

Invert the selection (choose Select > Inverse), then choose Filter > Noise > Add Noise. To increase the contrast, choose Image > Adjustments > Brightness/ Contrast. Slide the Contrast control from side to side until the desired effect is achieved.

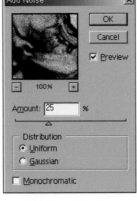

STEP 12

This part of our image is now complete. Now, transfer the head to the other side of this image. First, enlarge the canvas size. There should be ample canvas size, so we enlarge it to 2.5 times the width of the image. Before adjusting the canvas size, set the background color to white in the Toolbox

STEP 13

After adjusting the canvas size, select the white by Ctrl-clicking on the channel you created in Step 10 and inverting the selection so that only the image is selected.

STEP 14

Use the Move tool to move the image to the left. This will leave ample canvas space to the right.

STEP 15

The selection is still active at this point. Open the Channels palette and create another new channel. (This is to store the image's new position.)

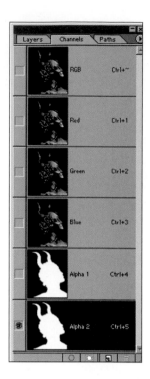

STEP 16

Return to the "Background" layer and copy and paste to create a new layer. Name this new layer "Drawing 2."

STEP 17

To flip the image, choose Edit > Transform > Flip Horizontal.

STEP 18

Use the Move tool to move the "Drawing 2" layer to the right side of the canvas. Set the blending mode to Multiply and the opacity to 100% so that we can see both the "Drawing" and "Drawing 2" layer on the background at the same time. (This is done so that we can verify and easily modify the position of "Drawing 2.")

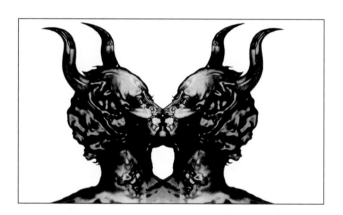

STEP 19

After the layers have been positioned, choose Layer > Flatten Image to merge the layers into one.

 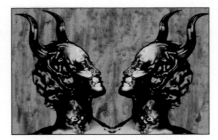 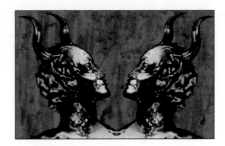

STEP 20

We've reached another mile-stone in this project's progress. As a sidebar to the actual project, here we have experimented with background textures.

STEP 21

We will now start working on Work 8 with the completed image that we have created. First, convert the image to Grayscale mode.

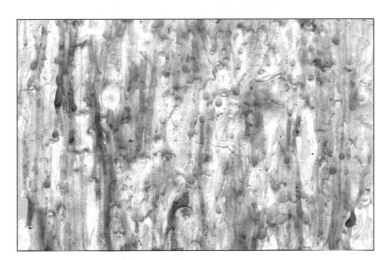

STEP 22

Create a new grayscale file. Now, add the image that will be used as the background texture ("Background01").

STEP 23

Name the resulting layer "Background" and leave its blending mode at Normal and its opacity at 100%.

STEP 24

We will now darken the overall background image. Open the Channels palette and after creating a new channel, open the "Background02" image file and copy and paste its contents into the new channel.

STEP 25

Convert the channel to a selection. Only the white areas of the image are included in the selection, while gray areas are partially selected.

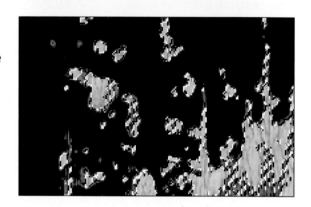

STEP 26

Go back to the Layers palette and create a new layer, naming it "Texture 1."

STEP 27

The selection remains active. Now fill the selection with white by choosing Edit > Fill. Then set the layer's blending mode to Difference and its opacity to 25% to 30%. We could have filled the selection with black to create a darker background texture, but then this layer might not blend smoothly with the other layers. The ability to stack layers with different blending modes one on top of the other is just as important as the painting and filtering itself.

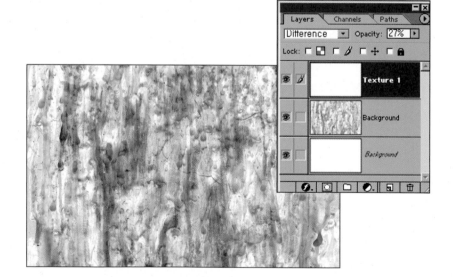

STEP 28

The center of the "Texture 1" layer appears darker than the sides. We will apply this same procedure to either side of the image to create a balanced effect. One option is use the Free Transform command to enlarge the contents of the "Texture 1" layer so that it covers the entire background layer. However, in order to maintain the details of the texture image, we will take another route. First, make two copies of the "Texture 1" layer and name them "Texture 2" and "Texture 3." These three layers appear to be empty in the Layers palette because they are all set to the Difference mode.

STEP 29

Adjust the opacity of "Texture 2" to 37%. Then use the Move tool to move this texture to the right, creating a darkened effect on this side.

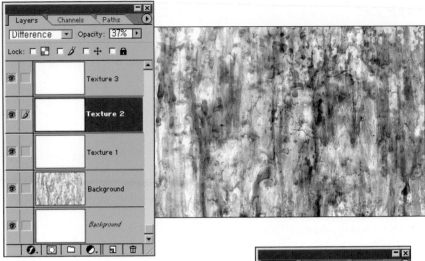

STEP 30

Similarly, adjust the opacity of "Texture 3" to 38% and then move it to the left side. Depending on the placement of these two layers on the background, a variety of different patterns can be created.

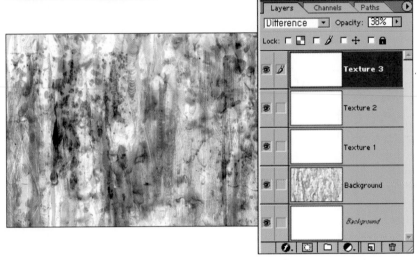

STEP 31

To soften the composite image, we'll add the image created earlier. Copy and paste the image's contents (excluding the white background) and name the new layer "Fog."

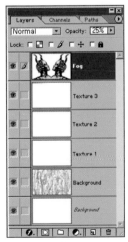

STEP 32

Set the blending mode of the "Fog" layer to Normal and its opacity to 25%. Then choose Filter > Blur > Gaussian Blur, setting the Filter Radius to 70. The texture now appears much softer than before behind the area covered by the two heads.

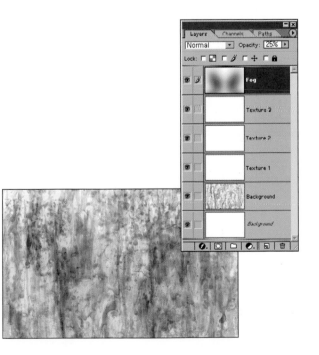

STEP 33

Add another copy of the head image. Because it was already copied to the clipboard to create the "Fog" layer, you can simply paste to create the new layer. Name this new layer "Original 1" and then adjust its blending mode to Overlay and its opacity to 43%. We will use the "Original 1" layer to create a butterfly-like image. From this point on, pay close attention to the state of the Layers palette as you modify portions of the image.

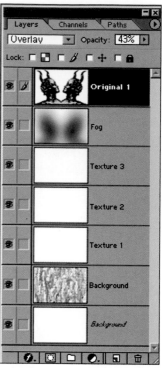

STEP 34

Now we will place the "Original 1" image on the background so that only a faint outline can be seen. This will be a good opportunity to see how greater detail can be added using a greater number of layers. First, apply Add Layer Mask > Reveal All from the Layer menu to mask the edges of the "Original 1" layer.

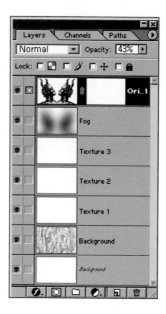

STEP 35

Press the [ctrl] key and click the "Original 1" layer in the Layers palette to select the area surrounding the two heads.

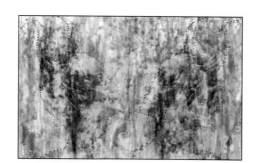

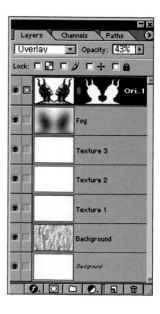

STEP 36

Make sure black is the background color. Give the selection a Feather value of 30 and then press the [del] key to fill the selected area with black.

STEP 37

Duplicate the "Original 1" layer, naming the new layer "Original 2." Adjust its blending mode to Overlay and its opacity to 80%.

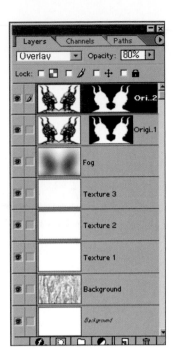

STEP 38

Place the "Original 2" image on the background as shown. Then, choose Edit > Transform > Flip Vertical to give the effect seen here. Switch to the Move tool window and use the arrow keys on the keyboard to adjust the position of the image.

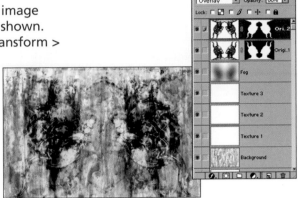

STEP 39

Because the images on the top and bottom were flipped, the background of the image on the top will appear brighter. Click on the layer mask for this layer to activate it and make sure that black is the background color. (Switch to the Marquee tool and drag a marquee select across the very top of the image. Then press [ctrl], [shift], and [alt] as you click on the "Original 2" layer in the Layers palette.) Set the Feather value to 50 in the Options bar. Press the [del] key to fill the selected area of the mask with black. This will hide the selected area on the current layer.

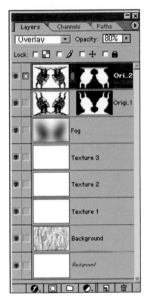

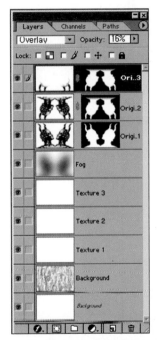

STEP 40

To add the original image piece by piece to the bottom of the composite image, make a copy of the "Original 2" layer and name it "Original 3." Set the blending mode to Overlay and the opacity to 16%. This will darken the image up the center. Then, while pressing the [ctrl] key, click on the image in the Layers palette to select it. Switch to the Lasso tool and set the Feather value to 30 in the Options palette, then press [alt] and use the Lasso tool to remove the top and center portions of the selection. Invert the selection and press [del] to remove the selected area from the layer.

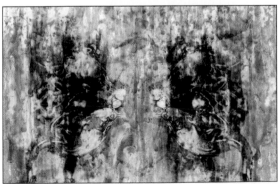

STEP 41

Now we will add some detail to the image. Make another copy of the "Original 1" layer and name it "Original 4." Set its blending mode to Overlay and its opacity to 60%.

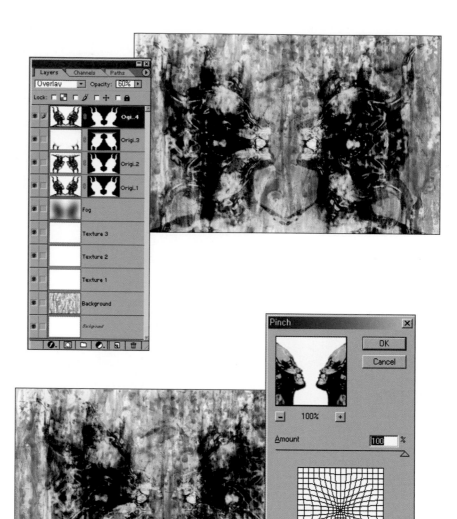

STEP 42

To distort the shape of "Original 4," choose Filter > Distort > Pinch twice to create the effect seen here.

STEP 43

The contrast in "Original 4" is now much sharper. Make a copy of the "Original 4" layer, naming it "Original 5," and set its blending mode to Overlay and its opacity to 83%. A sharper image will result. Pay close attention to this effect—there's a big difference between just using the Overlay mode and using the Overlay mode and adjusting the opacity at the same time.

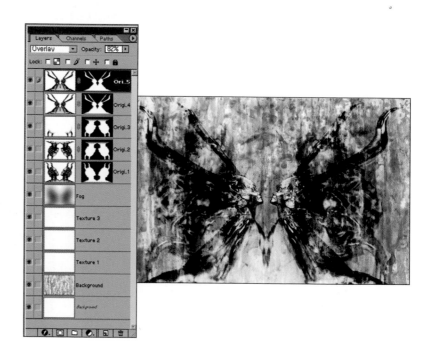

STEP 44

We will add some more distortion to portions of the horns of "Original 5." Use the Marquee tool to select the top portion of the horns and then apply the Pinch filter.

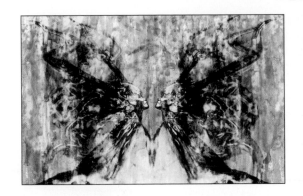

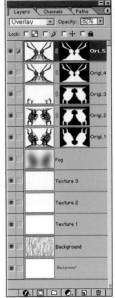

STEP 45

Make another copy of "Original 5." Set the blending mode to Overlay and the opacity to 43% and name it "Original 6." Again, choose Edit > Transform > Flip Vertical and use the Move tool to adjust the layer's position. Then, select the top part of the image and feather the selection with a value of about 30 pixels. Press the [del] key to remove this portion of the image. (Refer to the Layers palette.) There will be no visible difference from this step.

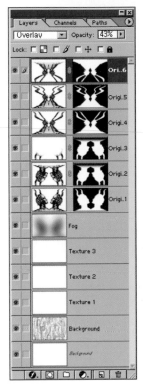

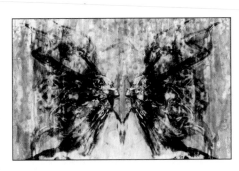

STEP 46

We will now add some delineation to the bottom portion of the image. Copy "Original 6" and name it "Original 7." The blending mode is then set to Overlay and the opacity to 30%. Using the Lasso tool, select the image, excluding the horns, and remove it in the "Original 7" layer. Although there is a small difference, the bottom portion of "Original 7," where the horns will be placed, is slightly darker. (Refer to the area within the red circles on the image to the right.)

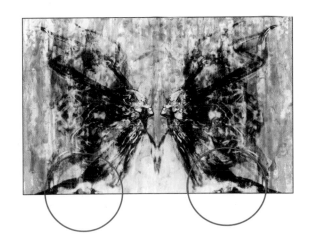

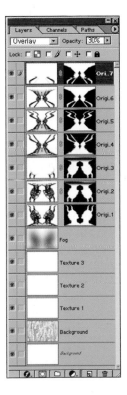

STEP 47

Each of the detailed and sequential steps that we took for this project has its purpose. Through this process, we can see that different layer filters and blending modes can give surprisingly unique end results. So far, a wing-like feature has been added below the horns in the image. Now we will emphasize the contrast between the wings and the background. We have a choice of techniques. We will use selections to create a soft band around the wings. Click on the "Original 1" layer while pressing the [ctrl] key to create a selection based on it.

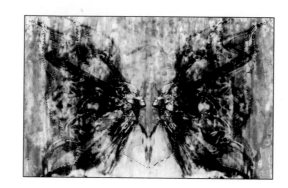

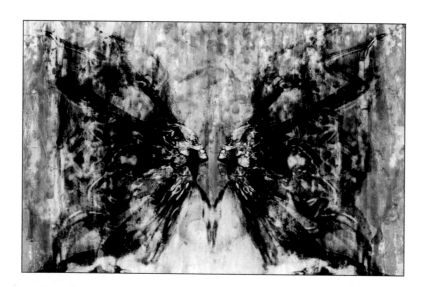

STEP 48

Create a new layer and name it "Border." Now we'll make a soft border the same shape as the selection. Choose Edit > Stroke and apply a 12-pixel black stroke to the selection. Then drop the selection and choose Filter > Blur > Gaussian Blur; apply a blur of about 8 pixels. Then adjust the blending mode to Overlay and the opacity to 100%. A sharp contrast will be seen near the wings.

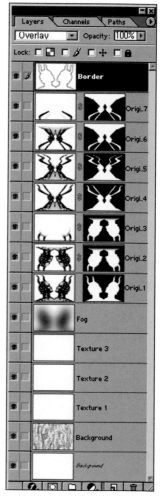

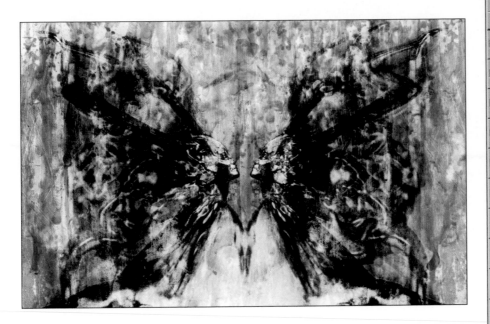

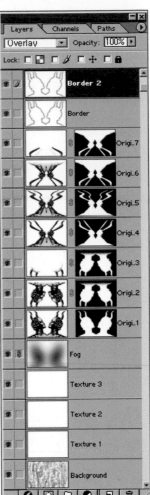

STEP 49

If the border seems too light, make another copy of the "Border" layer. A sharper effect will be seen. This concludes this project.

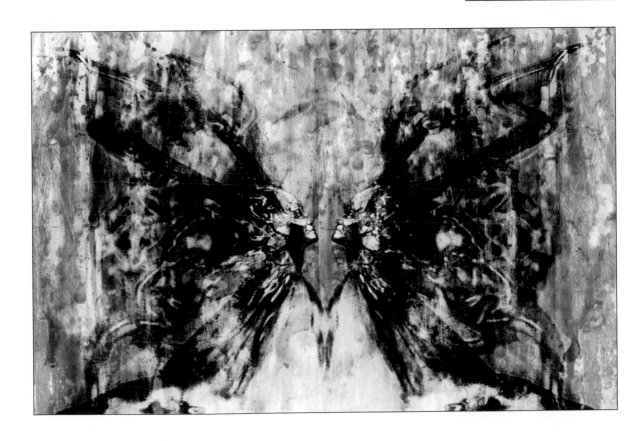

Project 9

Project 9 Source Files

Photo 1

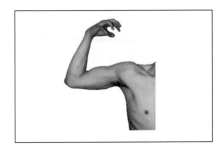

Photo 2

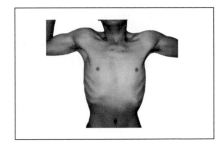

Background

Sky

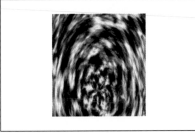

Cloud

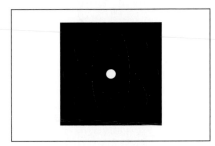

Line Diagram

Moon

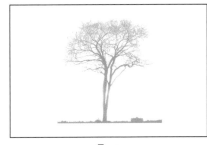

Tree

Look

Haha

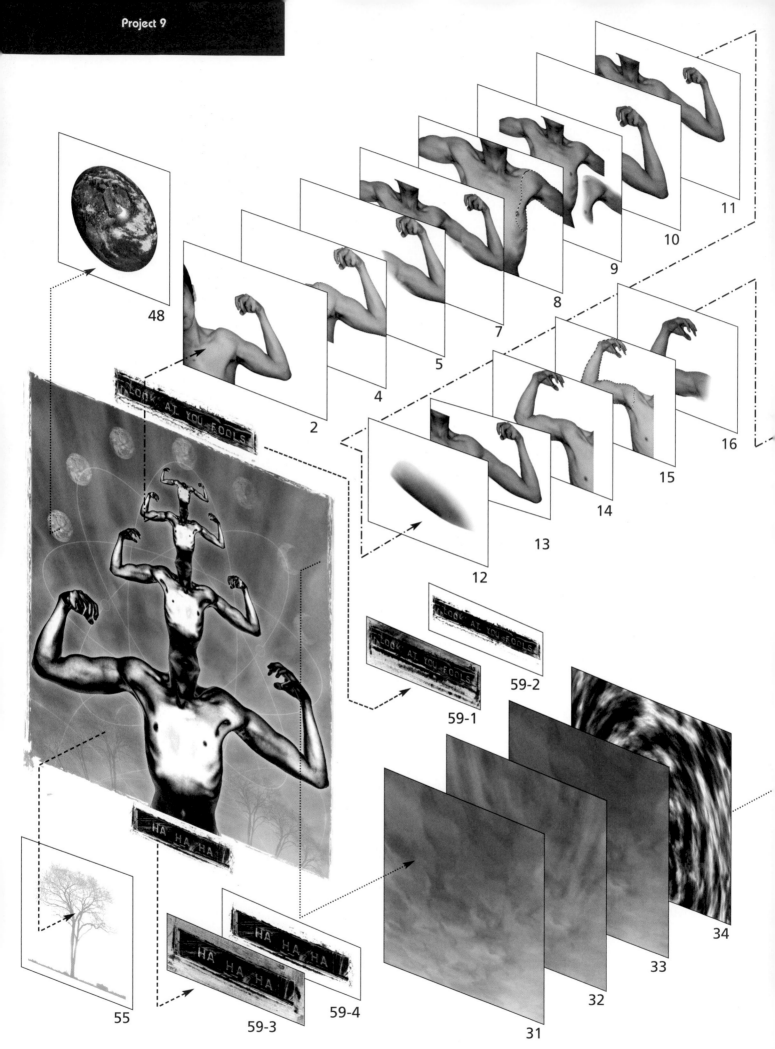

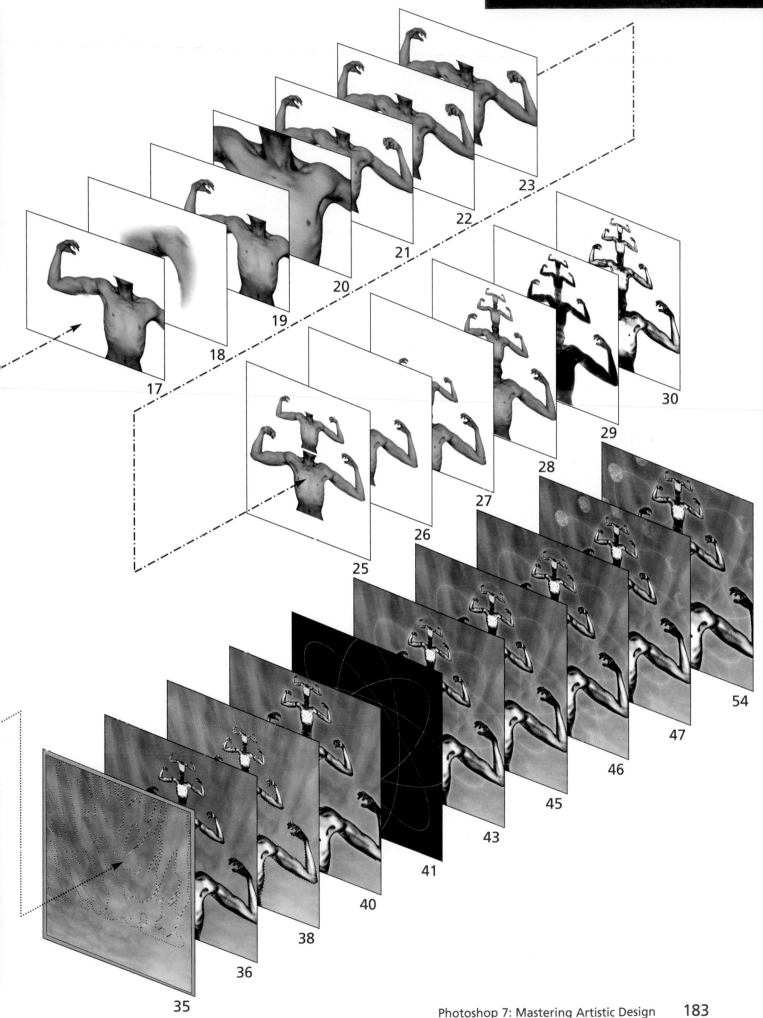

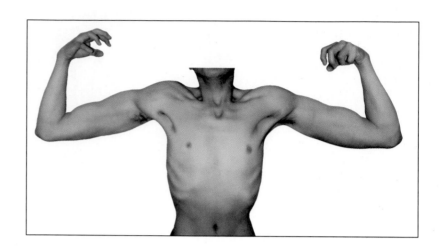

STEP 1

We'll start by creating the torso image that forms the basis of this project. The completed image is shown here.

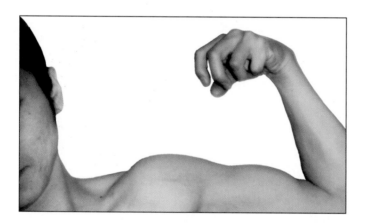

STEP 2

To create the image above, (first make sure all the component images are in Grayscale color mode.) Note that we will refer to the left and right sides of the image looking at the picture straight on; in other words, the model's right arm will be on our left.

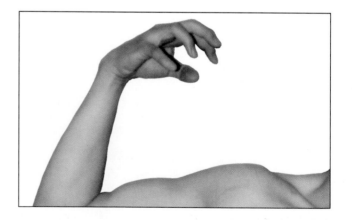

STEP 3

To create a deformed body shape, we will distort the arms and insert portions of an arm from another picture. First, decide on the picture that will be used as the base for this project. (You can start with "Background" if you like—just trim the arms and enlarge the canvas as shown here.) Next, we'll add the arms from "Photo 1" and "Photo 2" and create layers of different parts of each arm. (Refer to the images seen here.)

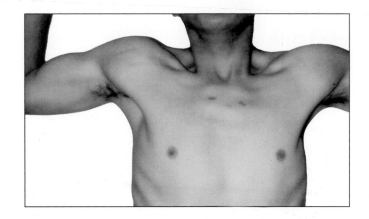

STEP 4

We are going to create a distorted and elongated arm. To do so, we will copy the arm from "Photo 2." Open the file and use the Lasso tool to select the arm and part of the shoulder.

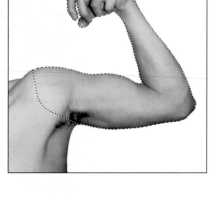

STEP 5

Once the selection is specified, invert it and set the background color to white. Press the [del] key to remove the background. Then use the Lasso tool to reselect the arm to the shoulder and (after adjusting the Feather value) copy the arm.

STEP 6

Paste the arm into the "Background" image. Name the new layer "Right Arm."

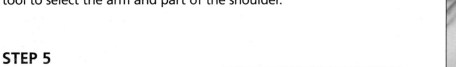

STEP 7

Now we will position this "Right Arm" layer on the background so that it blends naturally with the image.

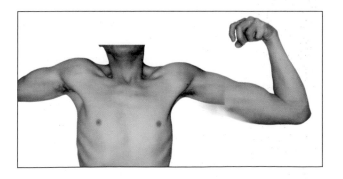

STEP 8

Because the thickness of the arms is different, we need to create a new armpit to connect the arm with the torso before working on the details. We'll copy and paste this portion of the torso from the "Photo 1" image. First, select the Lasso tool and set the tool's Feather value to 25. Then use the Lasso to select a portion of the torso. The image here shows the torso in the "Background" layer with the "Right Arm" layer hidden.

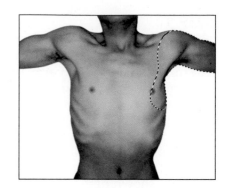

STEP 9

Copy and paste the selection frame. Name this new layer "Right Arm Extension." Situate the layer on the image and maintain its blending mode at Normal and the opacity at 100%. The image shows only the "Background Picture" and "Right Arm Extension" layers with the "Right Arm" layer hidden.

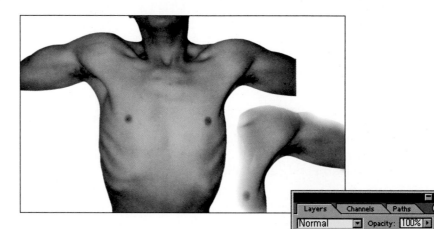

STEP 10

After pasting, the connection between the arm and the torso is still unnatural. Adjust the angle of the right arm and the right arm extension using Free Transform. For a more natural blending of the skin tones in the arm and torso, use the Clone Stamp tool. The image shows only the "Right Arm" and "Right Arm Extension" layers.

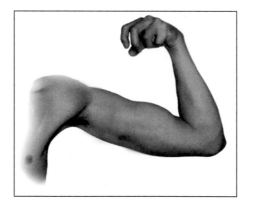

STEP 11

This image shows all three layers together.

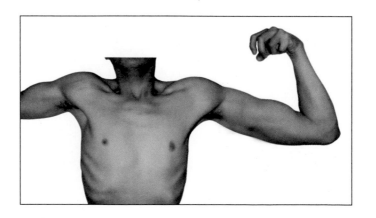

186   Photoshop 7: Mastering Artistic Design

STEP 12

The lower portion of the right arm still appears unnatural because it isn't shadowed enough; therefore, we copy and paste a section of arm that is shadowed over this area. The resulting layer is called "Right Arm Masking."

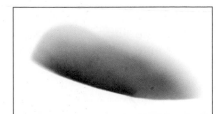

STEP 13

The right arm is now naturally connected to the torso.

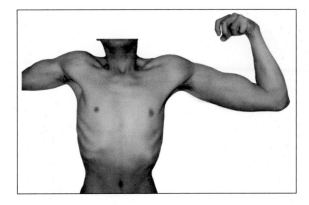

STEP 14

The left arm must be modified in the same way. Needless to say, it was not very easy to obtain a natural finish in the above steps. (Various source images and a close attention to detail are necessary to create a natural result.) To attach the left arm to the body, start with "Photo 2."

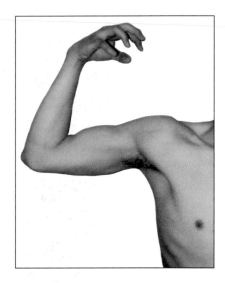

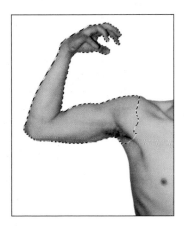

STEP 15

Select the portion to copy.

STEP 16

After you select the arm, apply Step 5 from above, finishing by copying the arm.

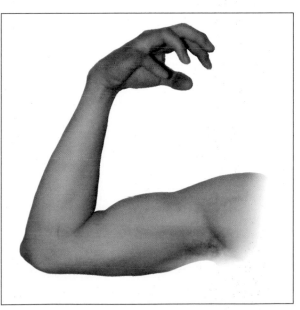

STEP 17

Paste the arm into the "Background" image. Name the new layer "Left Arm."

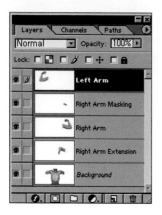

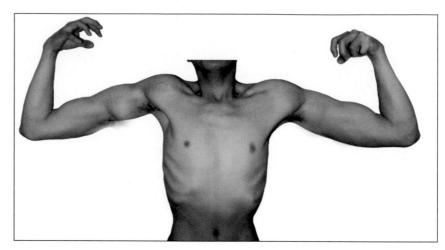

STEP 18

Now we will attempt to achieve a natural connection between the left arm and the torso. This process will be just as difficult as it was for the right arm. A middle portion is necessary to connect the left arm to the torso, so we'll copy and paste a portion of the torso from the "Background" layer. Setting the Feather value to 20, use the Lasso tool to select the portion and copy. Name this new layer "Left Arm Extension" and then use Free Transform to adjust the size and angle.

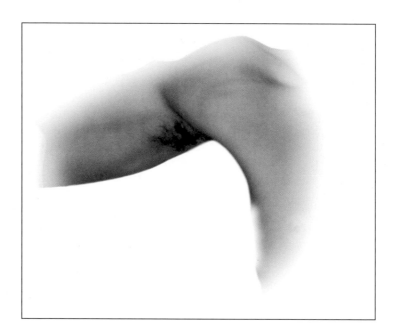

STEP 19

The image here shows the completed arms.

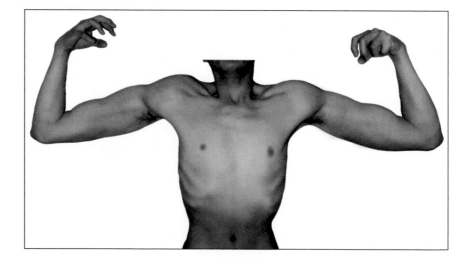

STEP 20

Now we are going to add another set of armpits to the torso and inboard of the existing set. To copy portions of the armpits, open the original "Background" image file again.

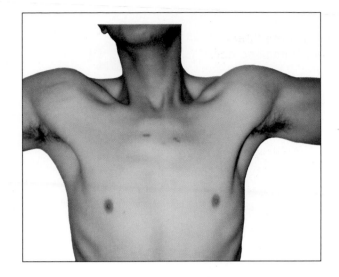

STEP 21

Select only the right armpit using the Lasso tool (Feather value = 10) and copy. Switch to the composite image and paste. Name the resulting layer "Right Armpit."

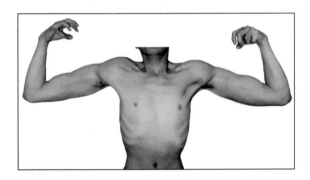

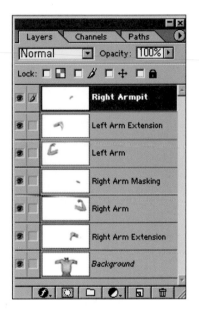

STEP 22

Create a left armpit as well. Although we could have duplicated the "Right Armpit" layer, we'll instead erase a portion of the "Left Arm Extension" layer to reveal the original armpit on the "Background" layer. Use the Lasso tool to select the left armpit on the "Left Arm Extension" layer and press the [del] key to erase it.

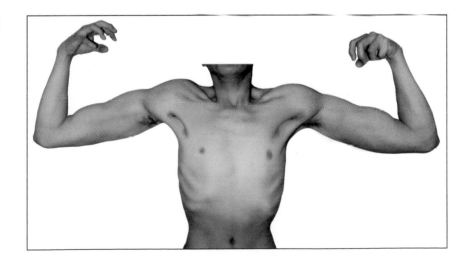

STEP 23

We will now add another set of collarbones beneath the existing ones in the image. First, use the Lasso tool to select the collarbones in the image and then copy and paste. (Set the Feather value to 20 in the Options bar.) Name this layer "Trachea 2" and position it below the collarbone.

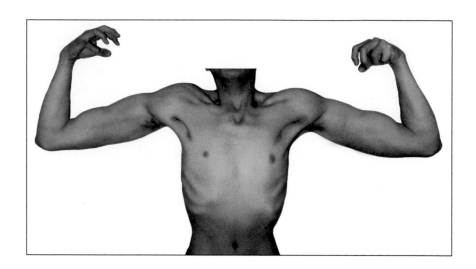

STEP 24

The torso is now complete. Before moving on to the next steps, here's a look at the image that we are trying to achieve.

STEP 25

First, because there are too many layers, merge them into one using the Flatten Image command from the Layers palette menu. To fit another image of the torso above the existing one, the new torso must be smaller and the height of the canvas must be increased. Once you've made this adjustment, click the white background using the Magic Wand tool and invert the selection so that only the torso is selected. Use the Move tool to place the selected torso on the bottom center of the canvas. Because the selection is still active, copy and paste and name the new layer "Torso 2." Use Free Transform to adjust the size of the "Torso 2" layer and place it appropriately on the background. Then choose Edit > Transform > Flip Horizontal.

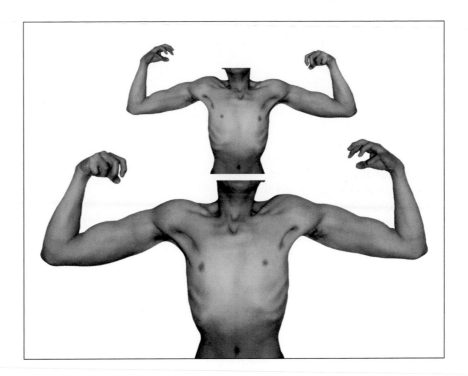

STEP 26

To create a natural blending between the two torso images, we need to think of a way to attach the two images. The area from the neck to the chin will create a very strange connection between the two torsos that is in keeping with the effect that we are trying to create. Select this area using the Lasso tool (Feather value = 20), copy it, and paste it. After pasting, name the resulting layer "Attachment." Then choose Edit > Transform > Flip Vertical. The image here shows only the "Background" and "Attachment" layers.

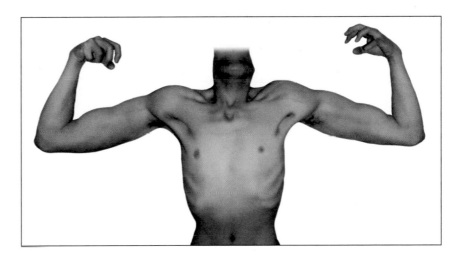

STEP 27

The lower portion of "Torso 2" must also be removed to create a natural attachment. After setting the Feather value to 25, select the bottom of the smaller torso using the Lasso tool and press the [del] key to remove it. The image here shows the natural connection with the "Background Picture," "Torso 2," and "Attachment" layers.

STEP 28

Repeatedly copying the images in this way will create the stacked torsos seen here. As we have already explained this step, we will forgo the specifics here. The topmost torso will be the smallest of them all and the head and neck should be removed after selecting with the Lasso tool to round the edge. The completed image is seen here.

STEP 29

We will now edit the image to make it look like a film negative. Use the Flatten Image command to merge the layers into one. Use the Magic Wand tool to select the white background and then invert it so that only the image is selected. Then choose Image > Adjustments > Invert.

STEP 30

Now we will add solarization effects to the image. With the selection still active, choose Image > Adjustments > Curves and adjust the curve to attain the effect seen here.

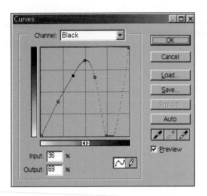

STEP 31

This object image is now complete. Save the completed image as "Monster Tower" and then close the file. Now we are ready to begin work on the project itself. Open the "Sky" image file that will be used as the background.

STEP 32

First, let's look at what we want the completed Sky image to look like.

STEP 33

Duplicate the "Background" layer so that you can experiment with this image while preserving its original form. Because the original "Sky" background is too weak for the effect that we are trying to create, we will combine the "Background" layer with the copy that we made. Name the copied layer "Background Copy" and set its blending mode to Normal and its opacity to 63%. When the two layers are combined, a slightly darker image results. Choose Image > Adjustments > Hue/Saturation from the Image menu and adjust the sky's colors.

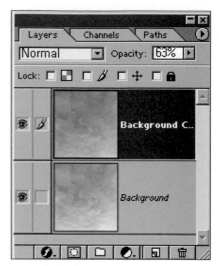

STEP 34

The sky is now slightly stronger. Now we will insert the image of moving clouds at the top of the image. To do this, open and copy the "Clouds" image to a new channel in the Channels palette.

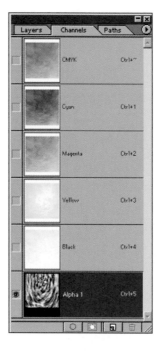

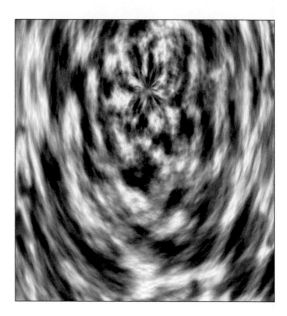

STEP 35

Create a new layer and name it "Clouds." Create a selection based on the image saved in the channel. Activate the "Clouds" layer again and choose Edit > Fill (setting the fill color to white). Then, set the layer's blending mode to Luminosity and its opacity to 30%.

STEP 36

Now open the "Monster Tower" file. Select the white background of the "Monster Tower" image using the Magic Wand tool and invert the selection (choose Select > Inverse) so that only the image of the monster tower is selected. Then copy the image to the clipboard. Switch to the "Sky" image and paste this copied image. Name the resulting layer "Monster Tower."

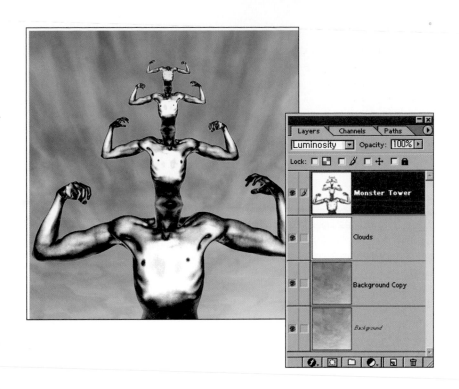

STEP 37

The contrast between the background and the image is too sharp. We will soften the contrast by adding a glow effect to the outline of the image.

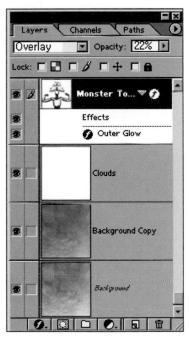

STEP 38

Click on the "Monster Tower" layer and convert it to a selection frame. (Choose Layer > Layer Style > Outer Glow.)

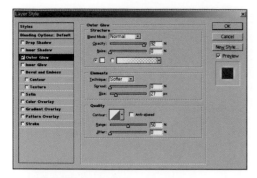

STEP 39
Adjust the values for Outer Glow in the Layer Style dialog box to create a slight glow around the monster tower.

STEP 40
The image here shows the effect of the Outer Glow style. We can see that the outline of the image appears slightly brighter.

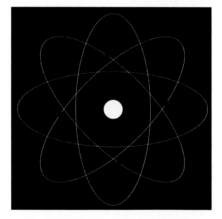

STEP 41
Open the "Diagram Line" image that will be used as part of the background for the image. Paste this image directly into a new channel in the composite image.

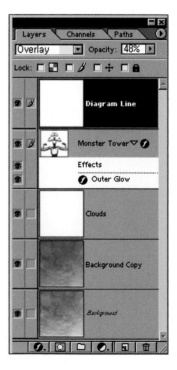

STEP 42
Convert this channel into a selection and create a new layer in the Layers palette. Name this layer "Diagram Line" and set its blending mode to Overlay and its opacity to 50%.

STEP 43

Create a selection from the "Diagram Line" layer and choose Edit > Fill (setting the color to white). The lines of the diagram will appear white. Because this layer will be used as part of the background for the image, drag the "Diagram Line" layer below the "Monster Tower" layer in the Layers palette. To create the effect of the lines spreading on the background, duplicate the "Diagram Line" layer, naming the new layer "Diagram Line 2," and create a selection from it. Then choose Select > Modify > Expand (setting the Expand value to 1) and Select > Feather (with a Feather value of 10).

STEP 44

Setting the layer's blending mode to Overlay and its opacity to 30%, fill the selection with white as we did for the "Diagram Line" layer. The lines of the diagram will appear to spread on the background.

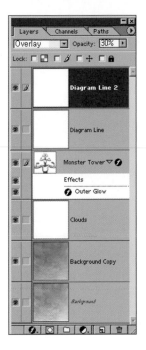

STEP 45

To create a faint image of the lines on the background, make two additional copies of the "Diagram Line" layer, naming them "Diagram Line 3" and "Diagram Line 4." Then, setting the blending mode to Overlay and the opacity to 30%, place one on each side of the image toward the bottom of the window. We will first place one layer on the left side of the image.

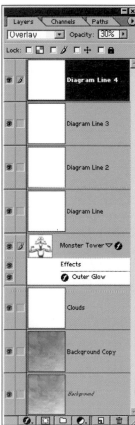

STEP 46

Place the other layer on the right side of the image. Now, let's take a magnified look at the entire image up to this point.

STEP 47

The next objects that will be added to this image are the equally spaced moons seen here arching over the image of the monster tower.

STEP 48

Open the "Moon" image. First, select the "Moon" image—which is actually the Earth—and copy it into the composite image. In the next step, we'll modify it to create a moon.

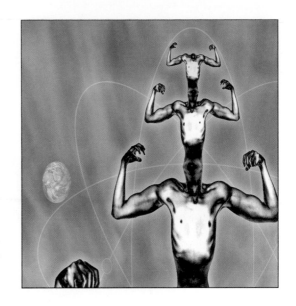

STEP 49

Name the new layer "Moon." To create a faint outline of the moon, set the blending mode to Screen and the opacity to 100%. Now the colors of the earth are faded so that it looks like a moon.

STEP 50

If we take a look at the completed image, we can see that the images of the moon grow fainter as we move from left to right. This effect can be created using layer masking. First, make six additional copies of the "Moon" layer and name them "Moon 2," "Moon 3," "Moon 4," "Moon 5," "Moon 6," and "Moon 7."

STEP 51

Set the blending mode for all of the layers to Screen Mode. To create the faintly dimming images, decrease the opacity for each layer: "Moon 2" = 96%, "Moon 3" = 77%, "Moon 4" = 61%, "Moon 5" = 42%, "Moon 6" = 39%, and "Moon 7" = 31%. Because the background for "Moon 7" is very bright, the opacity can be slightly higher than that for "Moon 6."

STEP 52

To change the forms of "Moon 4," "Moon 5," "Moon 6," and "Moon 7," we'll apply a layer mask to each layer in the following step.

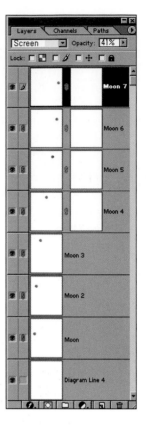

STEP 53

Starting with "Moon 4," we create a steady evolution to a crescent moon at "Moon 7." Click the Add Layer Mask button at the bottom of the Layers palette. Make sure that black is the background color and that the layer mask is targeted rather than the layer. Use the Round Marquee tool to make a selection to take a "bite" out of "Moon 4" and then press the [del] key to fill that area of the mask with black. This creates a crescent shape. You can copy the contents of the mask and paste them into a new layer mask for the next moon, then adjust its position to show the steady change from full moon to crescent moon.

STEP 54

The image here shows the completed work up to this point.

STEP 55

Now open the "Tree" image that will be placed on either side of the "Monster Tower." Select the white areas of the image and invert the selection so that only the tree is selected, then copy and paste it into the composite image.

STEP 56

Set the blending mode of the newly created "Forest" layer to Normal and its opacity to 50%. (Here, we are not trying to achieve the same brightness as the moons, but rather darken the image so that the contours are revealed.) Make two copies of the "Forest" layer and use Free Transform to adjust their size and position them as shown here.

STEP 57

The "Forest" image that will be placed on the left is complete. Use the Merge command to combine the layers and name the resulting layer "Left Forest." Because file size is always a concern, we must be careful not to create too many layers. To prevent unnecessary layers, combine layers with the same blending mode and similar opacities. If layers have different blending modes and opacities, they must first be modified before using the Merge command. For example, layers in Screen, Overlay, and Color Dodge modes and of varying opacities can be combined to create a specific effect that will be lost if the layers are merged. At other times, different blending modes are used to adjust brightness. At these times, the Merge command must be used with caution. Now the "Left Forest" image is complete. To create the forest for the other side, make a copy of the "Left Forest" layer, naming it "Right Forest," and choose Edit > Transform > Flip Horizontal. Then use the Move tool to adjust its position.

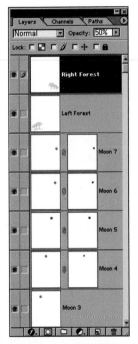

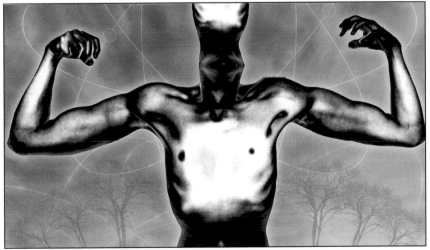

STEP 58

Merge the layers into one layer. Now, after setting the background color to white, enlarge the canvas size as shown here.

STEP 59

Now, load the scanned images, "Look" and "Haha," that will be inserted above and below the image.

STEP 60

Position the scanned images as shown here.

STEP 61

To complete the image, we modify the edges of the sky area by using duplicates of the "Look" image added in the previous step. Make a duplicate of the "Look" layer and adjust its size and shape using the Free Transform command. It should end up as a wide, shallow rectangle that runs along the top of the sky area but doesn't overlap the "Look" label above it. Then set the layer's blending mode to Color Dodge. This adds a bright edge to the sky area to create the edge effect seen here.

STEP 62
Complete the image by adding the same edge effect to the sides and bottom of the image.

Project 10

Project 10 Source Files

Background

Film

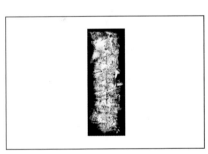

Clip

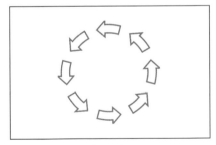

Recycle

Face

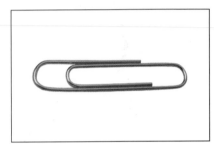

Edge

21-1

2

3

1

4

5

6

7

8

9

10

12

14

15

23-1

24

25

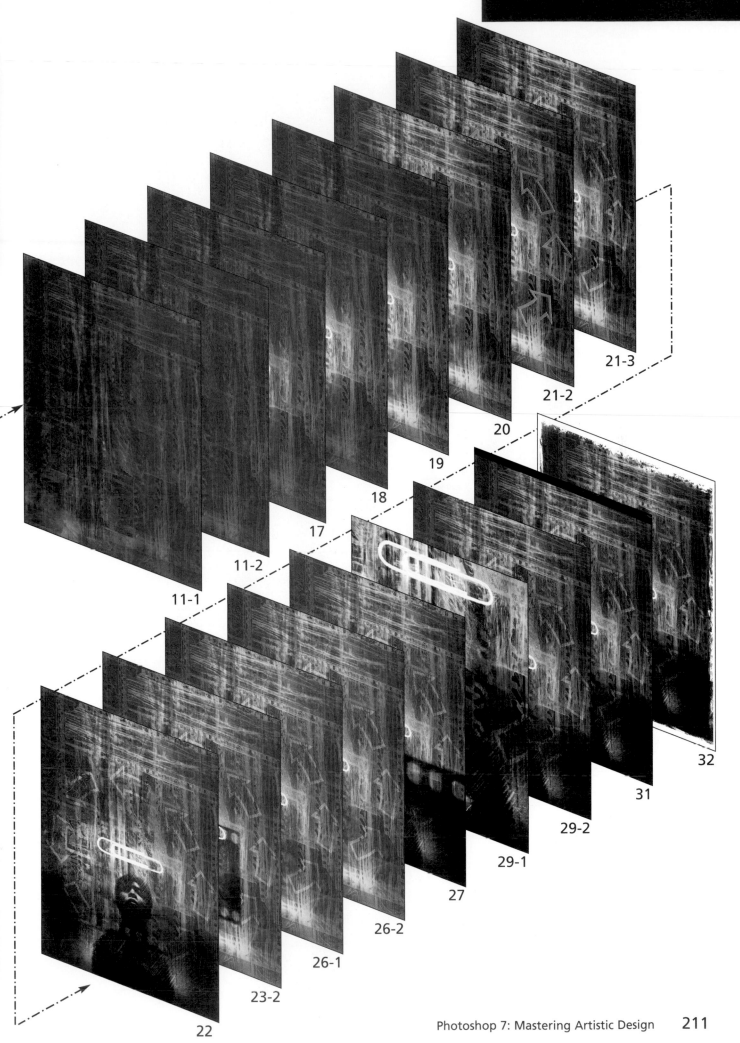

11-1
11-2
17
18
19
20
21-2
21-3

22
23-2
26-1
26-2
27
29-1
29-2
31
32

STEP 1

This project uses scanned film as its original texture. In addition, this project will introduce many other handmade textures. As mentioned before, handmade textures can be used to create a variety of different effects. We are no longer bound to the limited scope of Photoshop's graphic tools. The outline of the film used here was cut for texture and a sharp knife was used to etch a design. Untidy lines were trimmed using Photoshop's Paintbrush tool and the image here is the finished background. (The scanned image was reconstructed using Photoshop layers.)

STEP 2

Let's take a closer look at the process of creating this background. (You can recreate the steps starting with the "Film" file or skip ahead to the completed texture by using the "Background" image file.) A sharp knife was used to sketch a drawing on the film, and then the borders were randomly cut. The knife was rubbed across the surface, which was then scanned. The scanned image was loaded into Photoshop, and the Paintbrush tool was used to polish the image. The following images show magnified portions of this scanned image.

STEP 3

Choose Image > Adjustments > Hue/ Saturation to adjust the color to a dull blue as shown here.

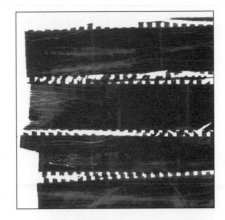

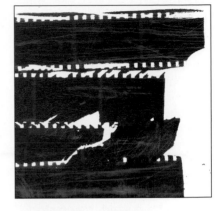

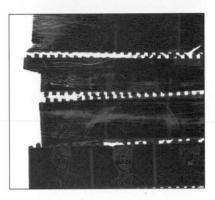

STEP 4

To create the background, portions of this image were copied and pasted onto random areas of the background. First, use the Lasso tool to select the bottom portion of the film image and then copy and paste it. Name this layer "Light Background 1" and leave its blending mode at Normal and its opacity at 100%. Use Free Transform to rotate the pasted image clockwise 90 degrees and position it as shown.

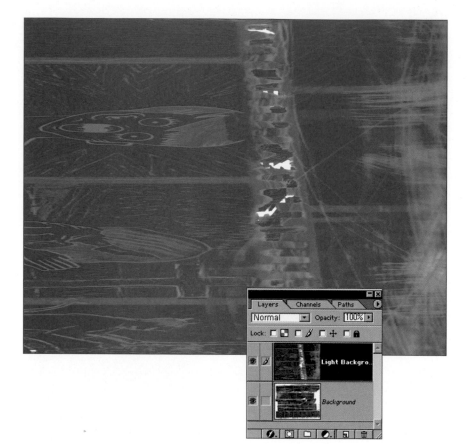

STEP 5

Next, make a copy of the "Background" layer and choose Edit > Transform > Flip Vertical to turn the image upside down. Move it to the lower left. Name the layer "Reverse" and leave its blending mode at Normal and its Opacity at 100%. The images here show both this layer alone and in composition with the other layers.

STEP 6

Copy and paste the "Background" layer again, this time excluding the white portions, and move it to the upper left. Name this layer "Background Copy 1." The images here show this layer alone and together with the other layers.

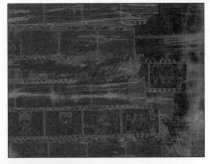

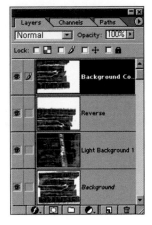

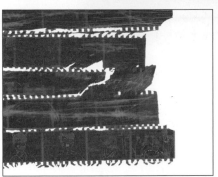

STEP 7

Make another copy of the background and name it "Light Background 2." This time set the layer's opacity to 43% to give an overall softened effect. The layers are overlapped in this way to create a full and abundant background.

STEP 8

The vertical lines of the background image are rather strong, so we will add some horizontal lines to portions of the image. Select the topmost fragment of the "Background" layer and copy and paste. Then use Free Transform to rotate it clockwise 90 degrees. Another linear texture will be seen. Name this layer "Horizontal_Left" and set its opacity to 63%.

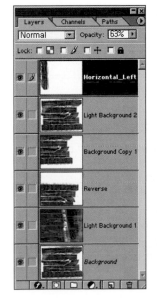

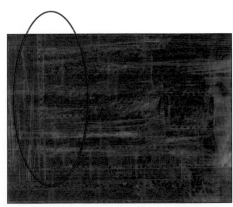

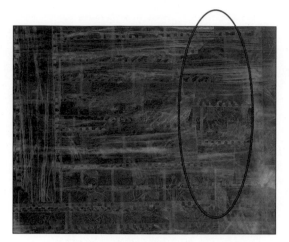

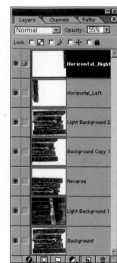

STEP 9

To add this effect to the right side of the background, copy the "Horizontal_Left" layer and use the Move tool to position it on the right side. Name this new layer "Horizontal_Right" and set the layer's opacity to 55%.

STEP 10

We will now add some scratches to the lower center of the background. To do so, make a copy of the "Horizontal_Right" layer and position it in place. Name this new layer "Deep Scratch." (Again, use Free Transform.) To give the layer a strong and bright effect, set its blending mode to Overlay and its opacity to 50%.

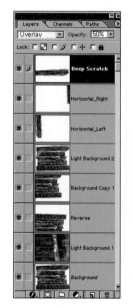

STEP 11

The background image is now complete. We will now use this background to finish our project. Merge the layers (or, if you elected to skip the background creation process, open the "Background" image). Before changing the background color, choose Image > Rotate Canvas > 90° CW to flip the vertical image horizontally. Then choose Image > Adjustments > Hue/ Saturation to tone down the color to a light brown.

STEP 12

Open the "Clip" image file, select the clip while excluding the white background, and copy it into the composite image.

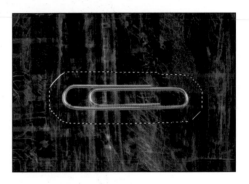

STEP 13

Name the new layer "Clip" and set its blending mode to Luminosity and its opacity to 100%.

STEP 14

To give this paper clip a neon effect, we will brighten up the surrounding background. First, create a selection from the "Clip" layer and choose Select > Modify > Expand to widen the selection frame. Setting the Expand value to 16, apply this command to the selection frame several times, until the selection frame triples to three times the size of the paper clip as shown here.

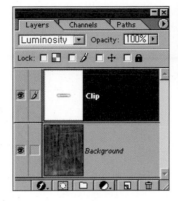

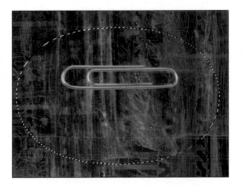

STEP 15

To soften this selection frame, choose Select > Feather (with the value set to 100). Then move the selection frame down a little bit.

STEP 16

Now we will lighten up this area. First create a new layer and name it "Bright Clip Shadow."

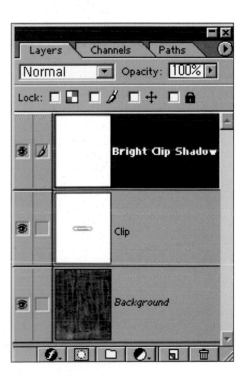

STEP 17

Choose Edit > Fill (setting the color to white). The interior of the selection now appears white. Set the layer's blending mode to Overlay and its opacity to 100% to create the effect of the light projecting into the background.

STEP 18

Because the light of this layer is still slightly dim, make another copy of the "Bright Clip Shadow" layer. Name this layer "Bright Clip Shadow 2" and set its blending mode to Overlay and its opacity to 56%.

STEP 19

To create the effect of a back-light on the lower part of the background, make another copy of the "Bright Clip Shadow" layer and name it "Lower Bright Clip Shadow." Use the Move tool to place this layer at the bottom of the background and then set its blending mode to Overlay and its opacity to 100%.

STEP 20

To create rays of light shining down from the top, make a copy of the "Lower Bright Clip Shadow" layer and place it at the top of the background. Name this layer "Upper Bright Clip Shadow" and set its blending mode to Overlay and its opacity to 81%.

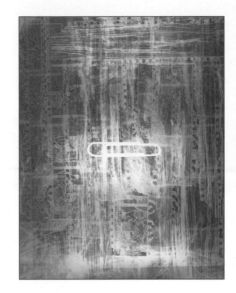

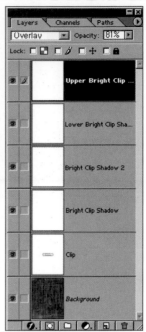

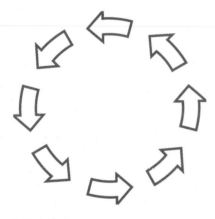

STEP 21

Now open the "Recycle" image, which will be placed at the center of the background. Select the non-white areas of this image, copy, and paste them into the composite image. Name the resulting layer "Recycle" and set its blending mode to Overlay and its opacity to 100%. This will again create the effect of light projecting into the background. The images here show the difference between when the "Recycle" image is first added and after the Overlay mode is applied. To create the effect of the "Recycle" layer fading into the background, place it below the "Clip" layer in the Layers palette.

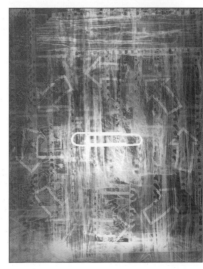

STEP 22

Let's take some time to look at the completed project.

STEP 23

Open the "Face" image, copy it (excluding the white areas), and paste it into the composite image, positioning it at the bottom. Name the resulting layer "Face." To blend it softly with the background, set the layer's blending mode to Multiply and its opacity to 100%. Place this "Face" layer below the "Recycle" layer to bring it closer to the background.

STEP 24

The roughened film border is too strong around the face, so we will use a layer mask to soften its effect. First, click on the "Face" layer and choose Layer > Add Layer Mask > Reveal All. Check the Layers palette to make sure the mask is targeted (rather than the layer itself), and then select the outline of the face using the Lasso tool, then invert the selection.

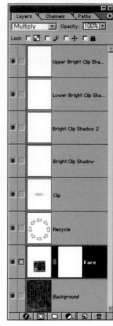

STEP 25

To create a softened effect, apply a Feather value of 30 to the selection. Make sure that black is the background color and then press the [del] key to fill the selected area of the mask with black. (As mentioned earlier, black areas of the mask block those portions of the layer from view.)

STEP 26

If we want to remove the mask, we can drag its icon to the Trash button on the Layers palette. A dialog box will then appear asking us if we wish to apply the mask effect before deleting the mask. Clicking Apply applies the mask effect to the layer. For this example, we will just leave the mask as it is. Use Free Transform to slightly reduce the spacing on either side of the "Face" layer.

STEP 27

The face is now complete. To prevent the shape of the face from overpowering the image, we will create a dark and dim torso. First, make a copy of the "Face" layer and name it "Torso." Set its blending mode to Multiply and its opacity to 100% and use Free Transform to triple the size of the image.

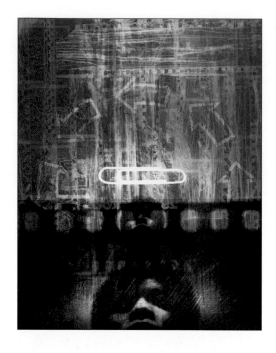

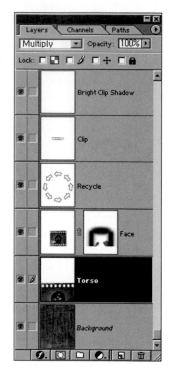

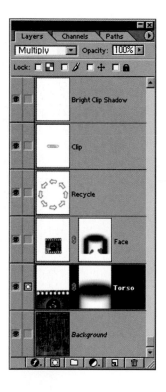

STEP 28

To remove the dark outline from around the torso, create another layer mask and then use the Lasso tool to select the area. Set the Feather value of the Lasso tool to 40 and press the [del] key to fill the selected area with black on the mask.

STEP 29

The "Torso" is the same intensity of the "Face" layer at this point. We will now transform it so that it appears more like a dim and vague shadow. Select the brighter portions of the "Torso" layer using the Lasso tool. (Set the tool's Feather value to 20 and the foreground color to black.) Then go over the interior of the selection frame with the Airbrush tool. The image of the face is hardly recognizable now in the "Torso" layer. Here is the completed image.

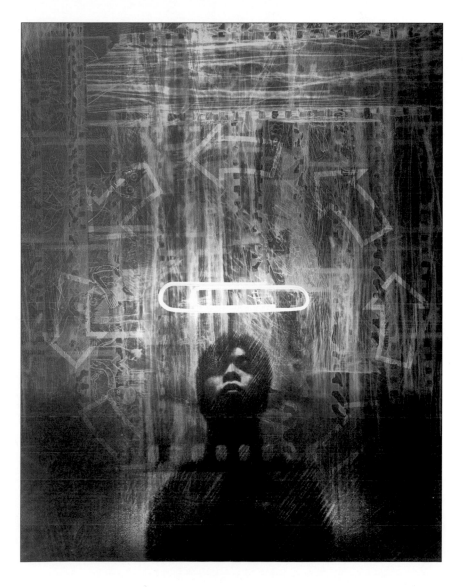

STEP 30

We'll put the finishing touches on this project by adding an edge texture. To do this, first open the image that will be used for the contour. Before moving this image into the composite, choose Layer > Flatten Image to combine all the composite's layers into one, then increase the image's canvas size to give it some white space around the edges.

STEP 31

Select the edge image and place copies of it around the four borders of the image. Use Free Transform to adjust the size and position. Name the four resulting layers "Top," "Bottom," "Left," and "Right" and set their blending mode to Color Dodge.

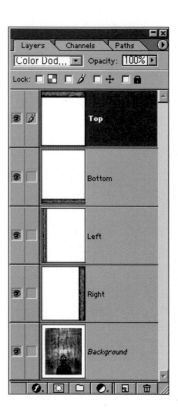

STEP 32

The border layers' opacity can be adjusted to the desired brightness. (Opacity 100% was used here.) In our version of this project, additional copies of the border layers were made and added onto the existing borders to add depth.

STEP 33

As mentioned earlier, to reduce the rigid lines of the edge and to create faint color towards the image's outline, we made copies of the layers as we worked. Each layer copy was set to a blending mode of Color Dodge and an opacity of 50%. The completed image is seen here.

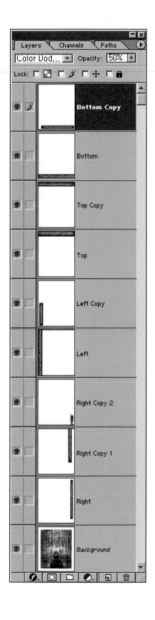

Project 11

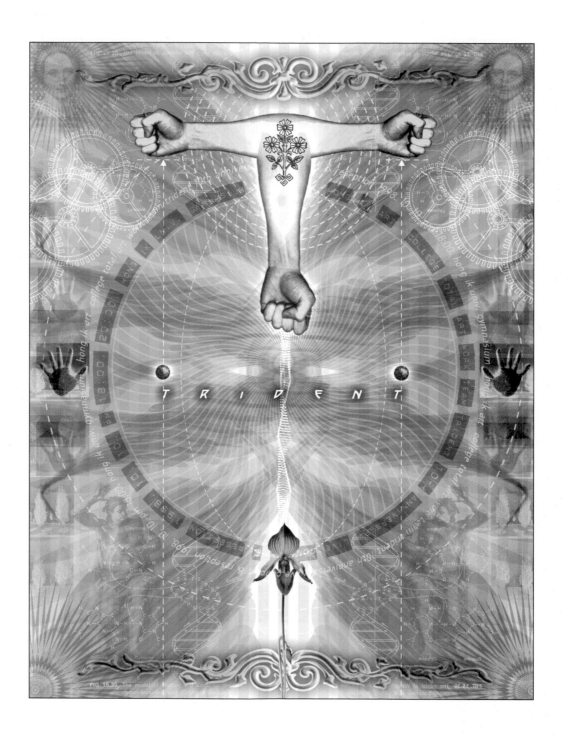

Project 11 Source Files

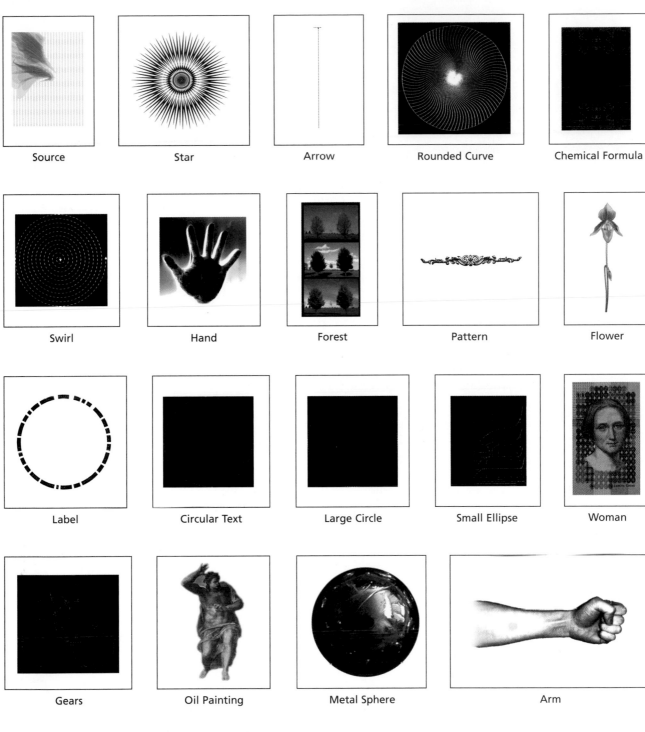

Source	Star	Arrow	Rounded Curve	Chemical Formula
Swirl	Hand	Forest	Pattern	Flower
Label	Circular Text	Large Circle	Small Ellipse	Woman
Gears	Oil Painting	Metal Sphere	Arm	

Light Beam   Tattoo

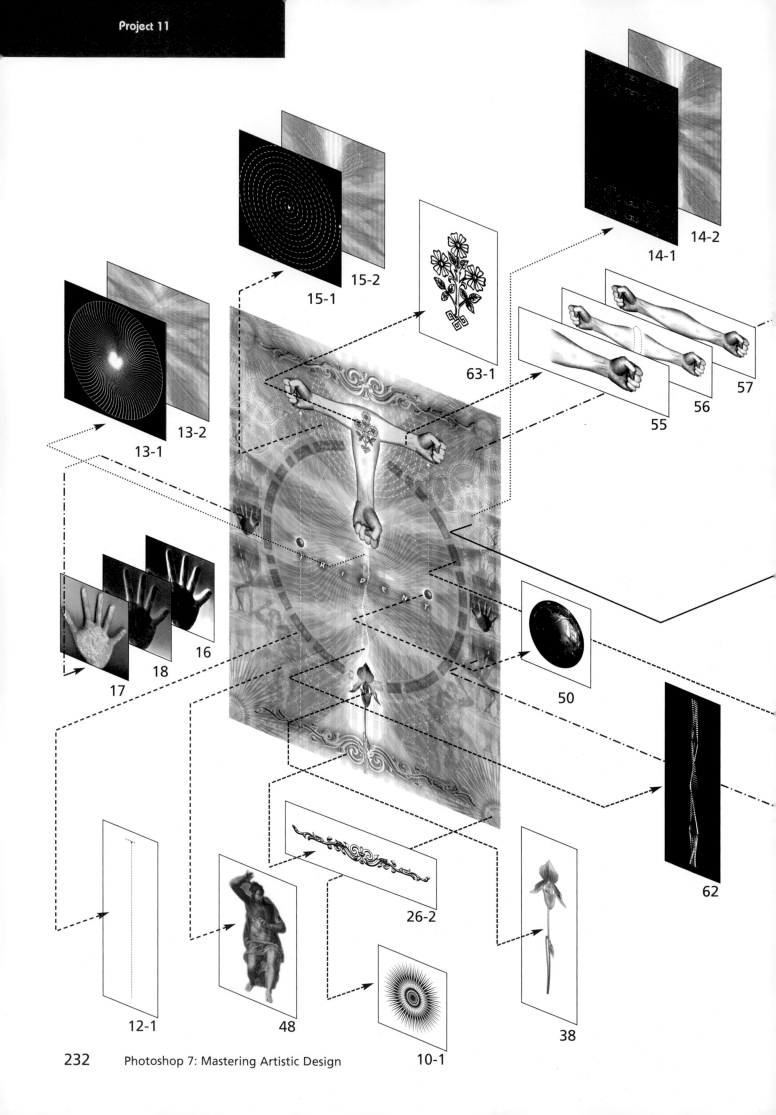

14-2

14-1

15-2

15-1

63-1

57

56

55

13-2

13-1

16

18

17

50

62

12-1

48

26-2

38

10-1

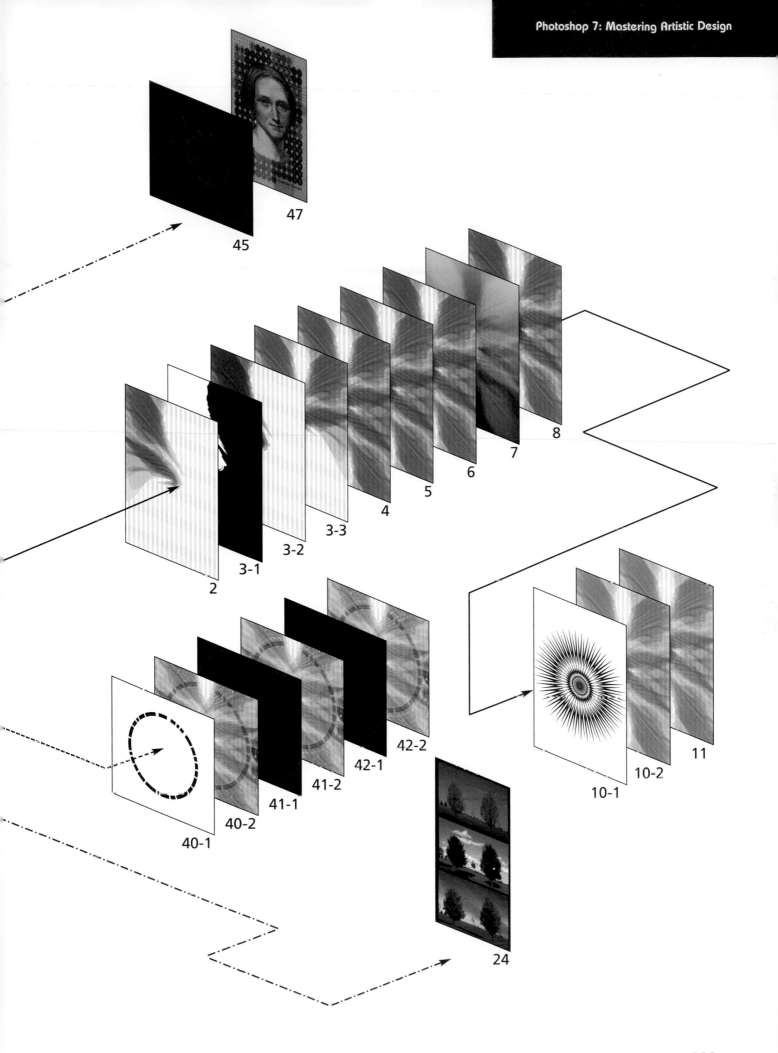

47

45

8

7

6

5

4

3-3

3-2

3-1

2

11

10-2

10-1

42-2

42-1

41-2

41-1

40-2

40-1

24

Introduction

Of all the projects in this book, this project is the most complex. Apart from the sheer number of layers it entails, each layer is a detailed work unto itself. To achieve the mood and color of the project, we used the Duotone color mode. This also helped to save a lot of time that would otherwise have been spent in adjusting different elements' colors to match each other.

This project was created as a poster for the 10-year commemorative concert of a college band. The arms, the focal image for this project, were used to form the letter "T" (for the name of the group, Trident). This was effective in conveying the powerful and explosive mood of hard rock. The image as a whole was softened to give a rhythmic feel to the surface. The circle in the center of the poster was created as a space for printing information about the concert, and the hands on either side represent the number 10.

Because this project involves many layers, we will skim over many basic steps, assuming that the user has gained an understanding of our methods from previous works in this book. With the exception of the background's creation, all the steps of this project are the same and involve the simple opening of images, turning them into layers in the composite image, and adjusting the layers' blending modes and opacities.

STEP 1

First, let's take a look at the background image that we are trying to create.

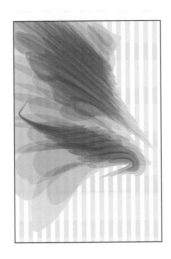

STEP 2

To create this background, we first need to open the "Source" image. This image was created using Fractal Design® Expression®, a drawing program from Creature House.

STEP 3

Use the Lasso tool to select the wing-like structure at the top left of the image. Save the selection as a channel and then convert it back into a selection. Click on the layer name in the Layers palette, then copy and paste and name the resulting new layer "Wing 2." Set the layer's blending mode to Multiply and its opacity to 100%. Now, choose Edit > Transform > Flip Horizontal and position the layer as shown.

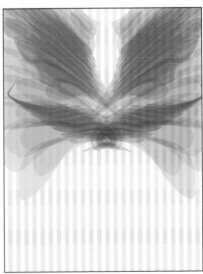

STEP 4

Now we'll continue to make copies of the "Wing 2" layer and position them on all four corners of the background as shown. Make a copy of the "Wing 2" layer, name it "Wing 3," and then choose Edit > Transform > Flip Vertical to position it on the right.

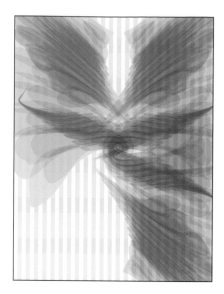

STEP 5

Make a copy of the "Wing 3" layer, naming it "Wing 4," and then choose Edit > Transform > Flip Horizontal to position it on the left.

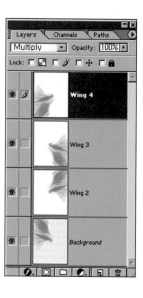

STEP 6

The basic background is now complete. The wing on the top left is fainter than the others, so begin to adjust it by converting the channel you saved earlier into a selection. In the "Background" layer, copy and paste the wing again and call the new layer "Wing 5." Set the layer's blending to Normal and adjust its opacity to 25% so that the pattern is more prominent, then adjust the layer's color and brightness so that this wing does not stand out from the other wings.

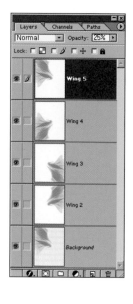

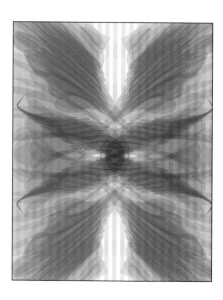

STEP 7

The image shown here is an experiment with color that we conducted on the side. After merging the layers using Flatten Image, we applied the Invert command and adjusted the image's curve to modify its color. Note: This is not part of the original project.

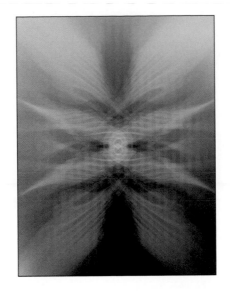

STEP 8

Before we begin adding objects to the composite image, we first change its color from blue to light brown. First, choose Image > Mode > Grayscale; then choose Image > Mode > Duotone. The Duotone Options dialog box is seen here. Choose the specified brown color and click OK to apply this mode.

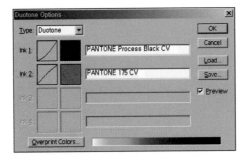

STEP 9

A light brown tone has been applied to the image. Before we continue, we will take a look at the finished project.

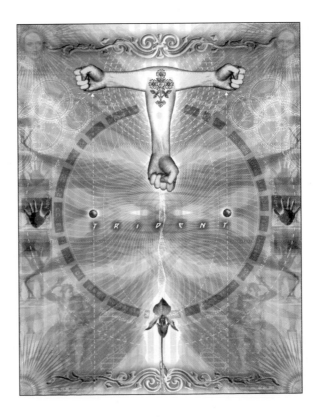

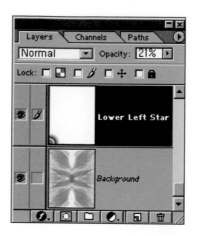

STEP 10

Open the "Star" image file, which will become the first layer of this project. Choose Select > Color Range to select the black portions of this image. Then, copy and paste the image into the background file. (The rest of the objects in this project will be added to the file in the same manner, so we'll refrain from repeating this step.) To prevent the darkening of the background, set the new layer's opacity to 21%. Move the image to the lower left corner of the background. Name this layer "Lower Left Star."

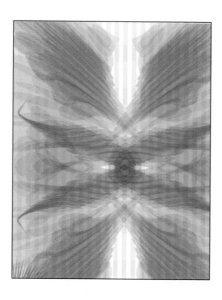

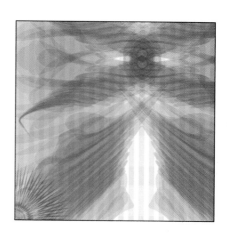

STEP 11

Duplicate this layer and place it on the lower right. Name the new layer "Lower Right Star."

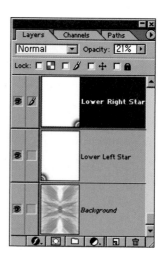

STEP 12

We will now add the "Arrow" image, which divides the background into three parts: left, right, and center. Set the layer's blending mode to Color Dodge and its opacity to 90% and then choose Image > Adjustments > Invert. Copy this layer, position the two lines as shown, and name the two layers "Left Vertical Line" and "Right Vertical Line," respectively.

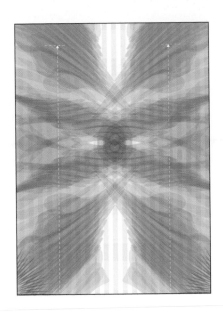

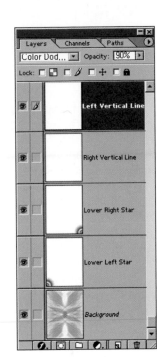

STEP 13

To create a vortex to the center of the background, add the "Rounded Curve" image. Name the layer "Central Weather Vane" and, to create a lightly projecting effect, set the blending mode to Overlay and the opacity to 25%. When a white image with a black background uses the Color Dodge mode (as the arrow layers do), the black background disappears and only the white lines show, but this isn't the case with other blending modes. Therefore, in this case (where we want to blend in Overlay mode), we first paste the entire image into a channel and then convert it to a selection. Then, setting the Foreground color to white, we use the Fill command to create the white pattern shown.

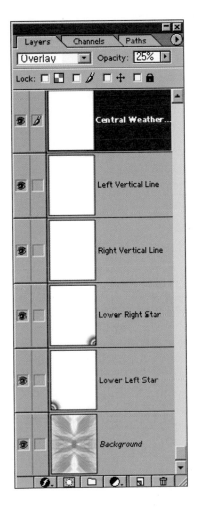

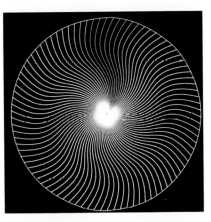

STEP 14

Add the "Chemical Formula" image, which will be used as a light texture on the background. Copy only the white portions of the chemical formula, excluding its background, and position it as shown here, setting the blend mode to Overlay and the opacity to 100%.

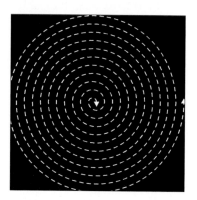

STEP 15

Next, copy the "Swirl" image that will be placed at the top center of the image. Copy only the white portions and position the image as shown, setting the blending mode to Normal and the opacity to 88%.

STEP 16

Add the "Hand" image that will be placed right center. Copies of this hand image will be placed on the right and left in order to represent the number "10." The image of this hand is blended into the background in such a way that it stands out from the other images. (This image is the scan of an actual human hand.) Name the layer "Right Hand" and set the blending mode to Normal and the opacity to 50%.

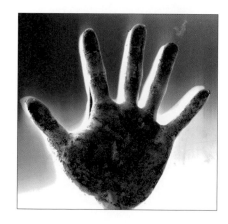

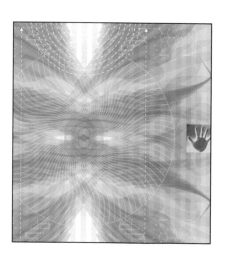

STEP 17

As a side note, here's how we created the image of the hand. First, we scanned a hand covered in plaster.

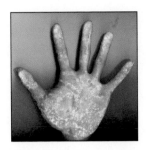

STEP 18

Then we applied the Invert command to the scanned hand.

STEP 19

The inverted hand was converted to Grayscale mode and the Curves command was used to sharply adjust the brightness of the image.

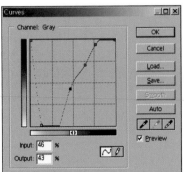

STEP 20

Now let's get back to the current project. For the hand that will be placed left center, duplicate the "Right Hand" layer and then choose Edit > Transform > Flip Horizontal. Arrange the left hand on the background as shown and name the new layer "Left Hand."

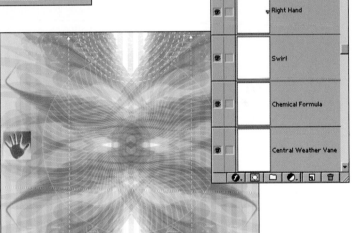

STEP 21

Now, we will duplicate these layers with reduced opacity and then place the layers above and below the original hands. This will create faint reflections of the hands. First, copy the "Left Hand" layer and place the duplicate below the original hand. Set the new layer's opacity to 17% and name it "Light Lower Left Hand." A light reflection of the left hand will be seen right below the original "Left Hand" layer.

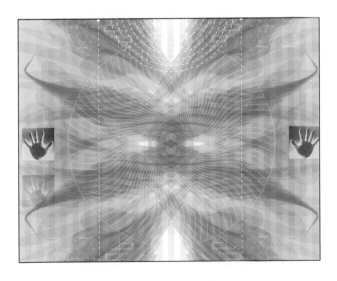

STEP 22

Do the same thing for the right side. Name the new layer "Light Lower Right Hand."

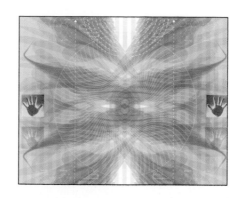

STEP 23

Now follow the same procedure to add faint reflections of the hand above the original images.

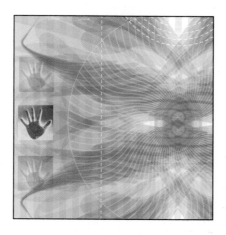

STEP 24

The six "Hand" images on either side of the background were blended with the background image by adjusting their layer opacity values. In the same way, to create a natural effect, an even lower opacity value can be used to blend other images. Add the "Forest" image, invert it, and set the new layer's blending mode to Difference and its opacity to 35%. Because we positioned it on the right, we will name this layer "Right Forest." Duplicate the layer and move the forest to the left; name this layer "Left Forest."

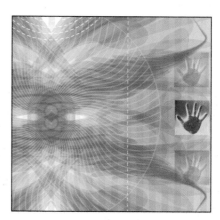

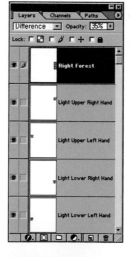

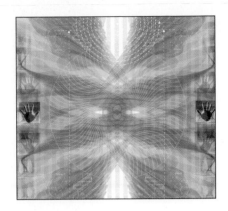

STEP 25

Create faint reflections for the forest as we did for the hand. Make two additional copies and position one above and one below the "Right Forest" layer. Do the same thing for the "Left Forest" layer.

STEP 26

Now we'll add some embellishment to the top and bottom of the image by copying in a clip art image, "Pattern." Name the layer "Pattern" and then create a selection from it. Choose Select > Modify > Contract and enter a value of about 5 to reduce the size of the selection, then save the smaller selection in a new channel. Name the new channel "Pattern." This is done so that a 3D effect will not be added to this portion when we bevel the background image later.

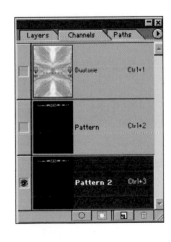

STEP 27

Light and shadow effects must be added to the 3D image. First, we will create a new channel that we'll use to lighten the interior of the "Pattern" image. Duplicate the "Pattern" channel and name the copy "Pattern 2." Then choose Filter > Blur > Gaussian Blur.

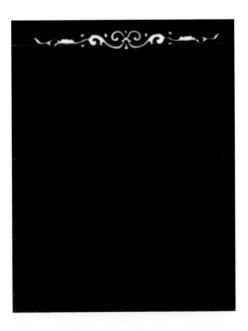

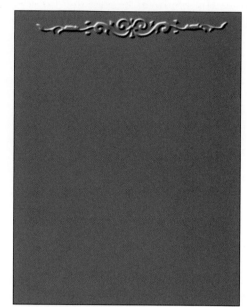

STEP 28

Next, choose Filter > Stylize > Emboss to add dimension to the channel image.

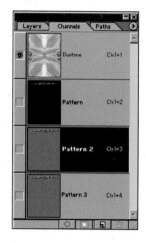

STEP 29

Make a copy of the "Pattern 2" channel and name it "Pattern 3." Go back to the "Pattern 2" channel and choose Image > Adjustments > Levels.

STEP 30

Click the black eyedropper in the Levels dialog and then click on the gray portion of the image. This will turn the gray portion black, leaving only a white shadow around the pattern. Then click OK.

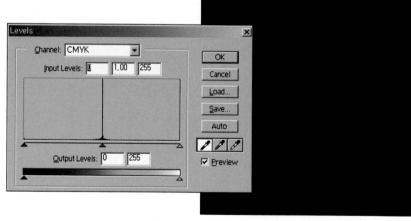

STEP 31

Now activate the "Pattern 3" channel and, returning to the Levels dialog box, click on the white eyedropper and then on the gray background of the channel. This time, the gray area will turn white, leaving a black shadow around the pattern.

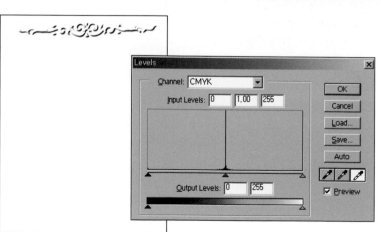

STEP 32

Invert the "Pattern 3" channel; later on we'll want to select the pattern itself, so it needs to be white on a black background.

STEP 33

The setup for adding a bevel effect to the "Pattern" layer is now complete. Before opening the Layers palette, create a selection from the "Pattern 2" channel into a selection. Activate the "Pattern" layer, open the Levels dialog box, and move the middle slider all the way to the right. The shadow of the design will be more prominent.

STEP 34

Return to the Channels palette and convert "Pattern 3" into a selection frame. Open the Layers palette and activate the "Pattern" layer, then reopen the Levels dialog box. Move the middle slider all the way to the left to emphasize the shadow.

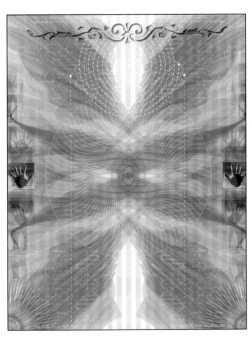

STEP 35

Change the name of the "Pattern" layer to "Pattern Top." Then set the layer's blending mode to Difference and its opacity to 60% to invert the shading.

STEP 36

To add more depth to the pattern, we will create a shadow around its edges. Make sure the "Pattern Top" layer is active and choose Layer > Layer Style > Outer Glow to create a black shadow around the pattern at the top. In the Layer Style dialog box, choose Normal blending mode and set the opacity to 65%.

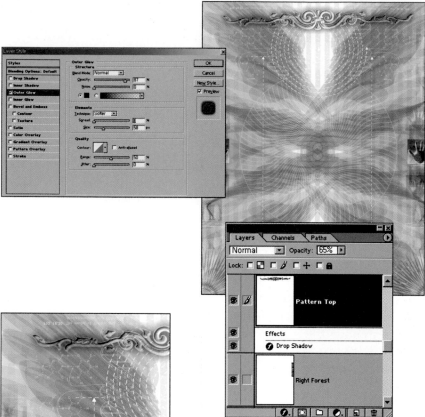

STEP 37

Now we'll position the same pattern at the bottom of the image. First, duplicate the "Pattern Top" layer and name the new layer "Pattern Bottom." Position this image at the bottom, aligning it with the pattern at the top. Then choose Edit > Transform > Flip Vertical. We can see that the shadow has been maintained.

STEP 38

Add the "Flower" image and place it right above the bottom pattern. Name the new layer "Flower" and set its blending mode to Difference and its opacity to 100%.

STEP 39

Because the flower and the bottom pattern overlap, create a mask for the "Flower" layer on the "Pattern_Bottom" layer. Create a selection from the "Flower" layer. Then activate the "Pattern Bottom" layer and click the Add a Mask button at the bottom of the Layers palette. (If you create the mask in this way, the selected area is automatically filled with black on the mask, saving you the trouble of doing so yourself.)

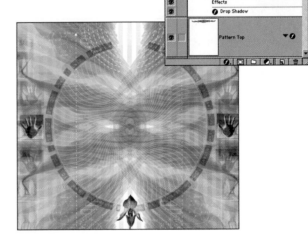

STEP 40

Now, add the "Label" image that contains the information, including the date and time, for the concert. This information was typed using the Punch Label font and converted to an image file using CorelDRAW. Center this image on the background, name the layer "Label," and set its opacity to 25%. This image also overlaps the "Flower" layer, so you'll need to create another mask. This time, make a selection from the "Flower" layer, then invert it before clicking the Add a Mask button for the "Label" layer.

STEP 41

Now we'll add another text image with the same text in a different typeface. Open the "Circular Text" image and then copy only the white portions to a new layer in the composite image. Name this layer "Circular Text" and set its opacity to 65% so that the text does not appear overly bright compared to the background.

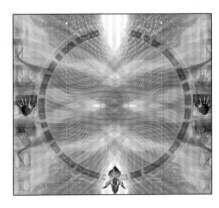

STEP 42

Now add the dotted "Large Circle" image so that it encompasses the "Punch Label" and "Circular Text" images. Copy and paste only the white portion and name the layer "Large Circle Center." Again, so that it does not appear overly bright, set the layer's opacity to 70%.

STEP 43

Make copies of the "Lower Left Star" and "Lower Right Star" layers and use Free Transform to adjust their sizes and place the stars at the top of the image as shown. In contrast to the stars at the bottom, set the blending mode to Hard Light and the opacity to 29%. Name these layers "Top Left Star" and "Top Right Star."

STEP 44

Open the "Small Ellipse" image and place it within the "Central Weather Vane" layer. Name this layer "Small Ellipse." Because the dotted lines are thin and fine, set the blend mode to Color Dodge to create a bright, diffused effect. Then adjust the layer's opacity to 30%.

STEP 45

We will now add the gear out-lines in the center of the image. First, open the "Gears" image and place a copy of it on either side of the "Large Circle" element in the composite image (note that the gears are rotated 90° from their position in the source file). Name the left gear layer "Gears" and its blending mode to Color Dodge at an opacity of 75%.

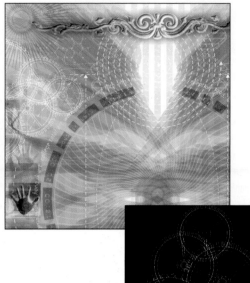

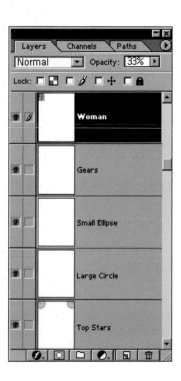

STEP 46

Duplicate the "Gears" layer and move the new layer to the right to create a reflection.

STEP 47

Now add the "Woman" image and place it inside the top left star. Give the "Woman" layer an opacity of 33%, then dupli-cate the layer, flip the dupli-cate horizontally, and place it over the right star.

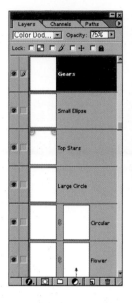

STEP 48

Detail has been added to the top edge of the large circle in the center. We will now embellish the lower edge. First, add the "Oil Painting" image, place it near the lower left edge, and name this layer "Lower Left Oil Painting." To create the effect of this image merging with the background, set the layer's blending mode to Hard Light and its opacity to 30%.

STEP 49

Duplicate this layer and align the copy in place on the right side as shown here.

STEP 50

Now we'll add two copies of the "Metal Sphere" image and position them so the spheres look as though they're suspended on the two perpendicular lines on each side inside the center circle. Copy and paste the image of the metal sphere and name the layer "Sphere Left." Set its blending mode to Hard Light and its opacity to 65% and center it on the left perpendicular line. Then position a duplicate of this layer so that the sphere is centered on the right perpendicular line.

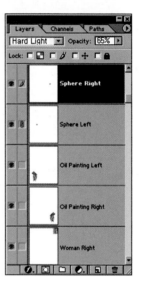

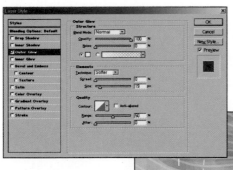

STEP 51

We'll add backlighting to the metal spheres to give them some depth. Select the "Sphere Left" layer and choose Layer > Layer Style > Outer Glow. Do the same for the "Sphere Right" layer.

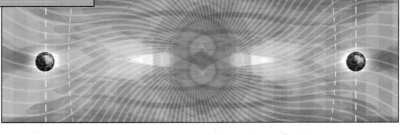

STEP 52

Next, use the Type tool to insert the band's name, Trident. Set the text color to white and position the lettering below the two spheres. Keep the type layer's opacity at 100% and its blending mode at Normal.

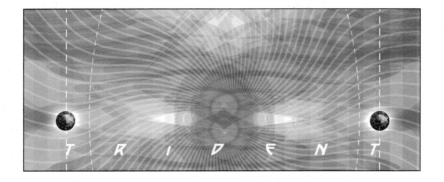

STEP 53

Now we'll add a glow behind the white letters to make them stand out from the background. Click on the Layers palette's Add a Layer Style button and choose Outer Glow. Set the color of the glow to black. Because the image's color mode is Duotone, the glow will not appear completely black, but it is still effective. If you want a greater contrast between the letters and the glow, experiment with different opacity and blending mode settings.

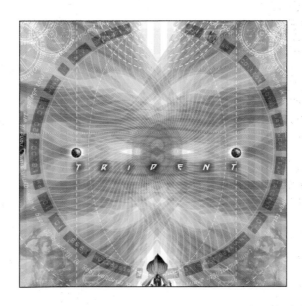

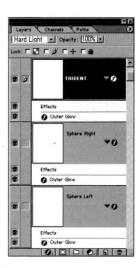

STEP 54

Next we will add the "Arm" image that will be used to form the letter "T" (standing for TRIDENT). Let's first take a look at the completed picture.

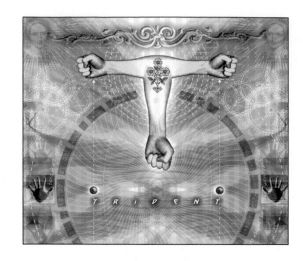

STEP 55

The construction of the T is a bit tricky, so let's work on it in a separate file. First, open the "Arm" image and duplicate the "Background" layer to create an "Arm 2" layer. (The "Background" layer here is the original "Arm" layer.) Choose Edit > Transform > Flip Horizontal to flip the "Arm 2" layer over.

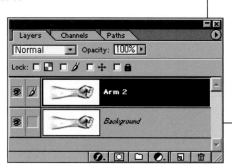

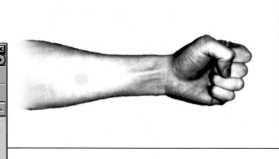

STEP 56

Before going any further, increase the width of the canvas to make room for the two arms. Now select the cut-off end of the arm in the "Arm 2" layer using the Lasso tool and feather the selection. Fade out the end of the arm by pressing the [del] key (repeatedly if necessary) and then bring the two arms together so they're joined naturally.

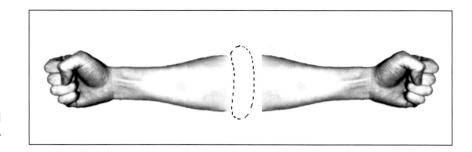

STEP 57

We have now completed the top "Arm" image. Save this file in Photoshop native format under a different name ("Both Arms") and then merge the two arm layers together. Then, after selecting and copying only the image of the joined arms, close the file without saving.

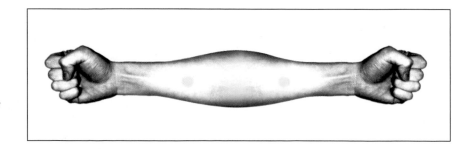

STEP 58

Return to the Duotone image created earlier and paste the copied image of the joined arms. Name this layer "Both Arms" and set the layer's blending mode to Normal and its opacity to 94%.

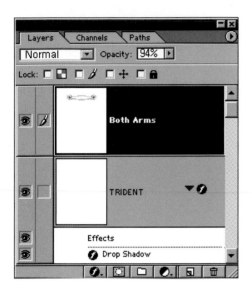

STEP 59

Open the "Both Arms" file and copy only the "Arm 2" layer. After closing the file, return to the Duotone image and paste. Name the new layer "Lower Arm" and set its blending mode to Normal and its opacity to 75%.

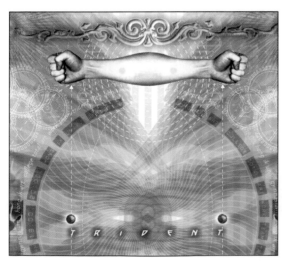

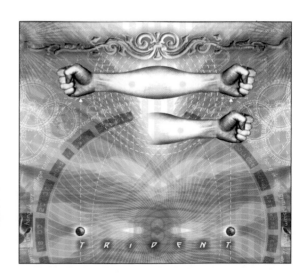

STEP 60

Use the Transform command to rotate the "Lower Arm" layer clockwise 90 degrees. Adjust the position of this image until a perfect "T" is formed.

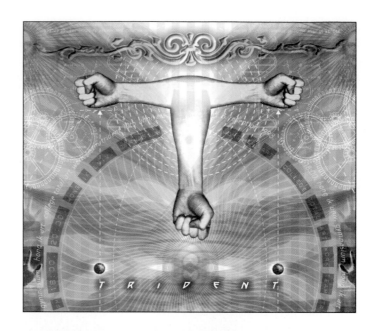

STEP 61

Click on the "Lower Arm" layer. Click the Add a Layer Style button in the Layers palette and choose Outer Glow to add a faint white shadow.

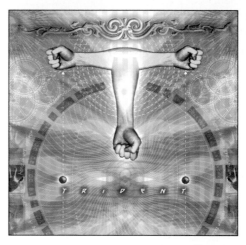

STEP 62

Now we'll create the effect of a light beam running between the lower arm and the flower image at the bottom. First, open the "Light Beam" image file, drag its contents into the composite file with the Move tool, and name the resulting layer "Light Beam." To diffuse the beam, set the layer's blending mode to Color Dodge and its opacity to 62%.

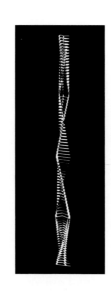
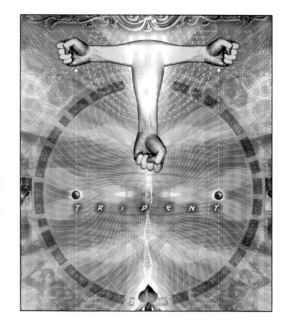

STEP 63

Up until now we have worked with a variety of blending modes and opacity settings to integrate the many layers of this project. Although the steps in themselves were simple, each step added a great deal of detail. These details are what add up to create the overall effect of the final image; therefore they cannot be overlooked. As a final step, we will add the image of the tattoo on the arm. Open the "Tattoo" image file and select its black areas. Paste the image into the composite and set the new layer's opacity to 60% (to keep the tattoo from looking too dark). This brings us to the end of this project.

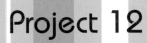

Project 12

Project 12 Source Files

Background

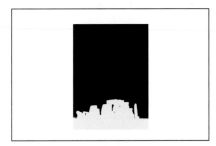

Mask

Stonehenge

Insect

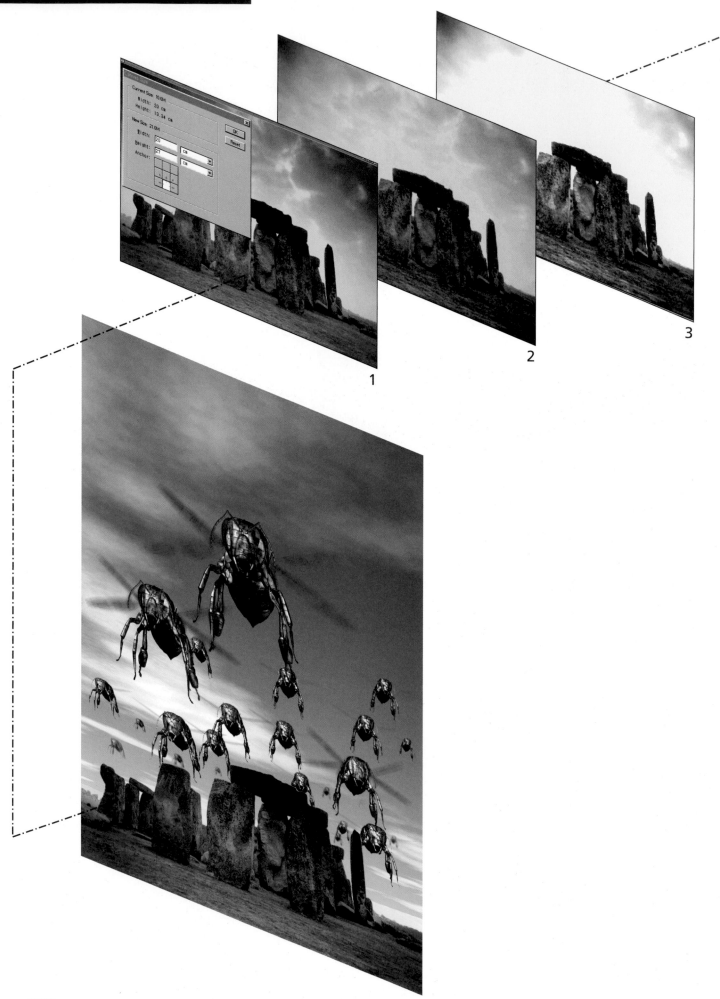

1

2

3

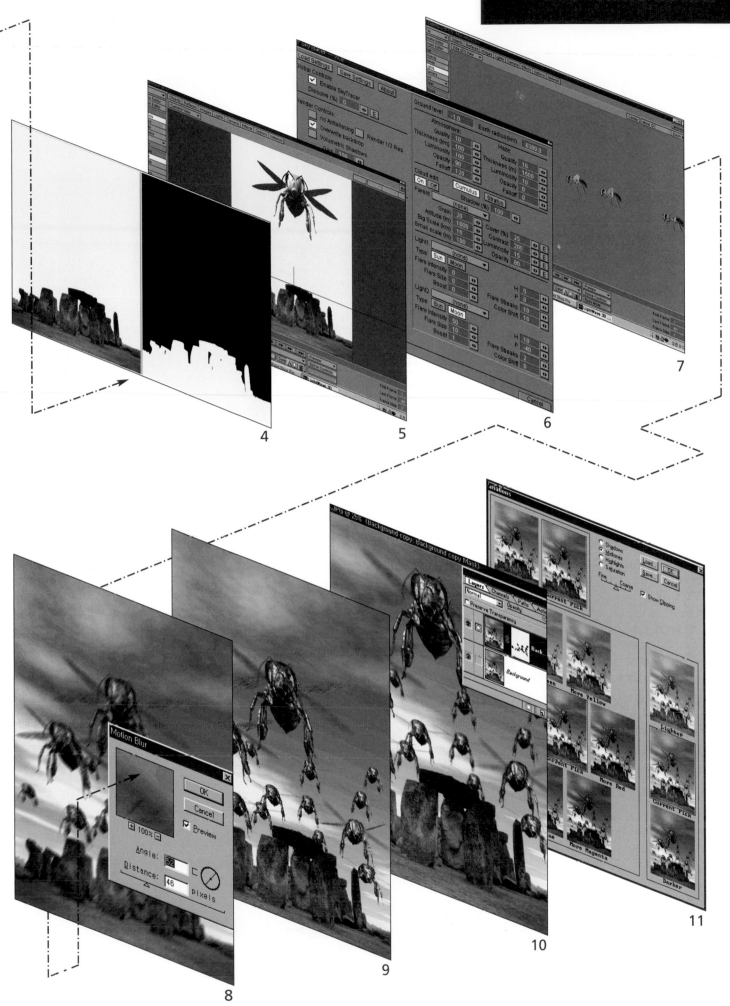

4

5

6

7

8

9

10

11

STEP 1

We start by opening the "Background" image and adjusting it to fit the purposes of our project. The Stonehenge image will appear at the bottom of the background, with much greater height of sky than in the original image, so adjust the size of the canvas as seen here. Then make sure the image is in RGB color mode.

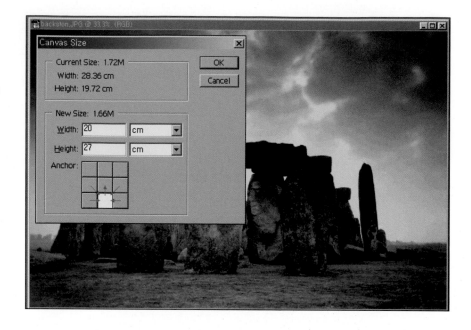

STEP 2

To delicately remove portions of the sky, we will use an alpha channel. Click on each color channel in the Channels palette until you find the channel that has the greatest contrast between the sky and the Stonehenge. In this case, the Red channel is the most appropriate. Drag the color channel to the Create New Channel button to create a duplicate of it; name the new Channel "Background 2."

STEP 3

Choose Image > Adjustments > Levels and click the white eye-dropper. Click on a midtone area of the sky. All areas of the sky brighter than this midtone will now appear white. Close the Levels dialog box and use the Lasso tool to select the darker areas of the sky, then fill the selection with white. Returning to the Levels dialog box, click the black eyedropper and click on the lightest area of Stonehenge to turn the stones black.

STEP 4

Click this alpha channel while pressing the [ctrl] key to load it as a selection, then return to the "Background" layer. Fill the selected sky with white using the Fill command. Save the image as "Stonehenge." Then invert the alpha channel and use the Duplicate Channel command in the Channels palette menu to save it as a separate document called "Mask." These two images will be used as the foreground and mask in a 3D program.

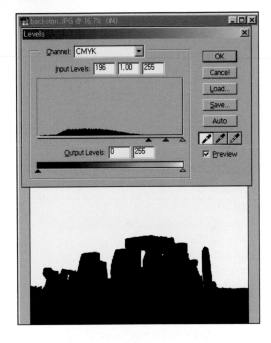

STEP 5

Open the "Stonehenge" and "Mask" images in the 3D program. (We used NewTek LightWave 3D.) The "Stonehenge" file will be used as the foreground image and the "Mask" as the foreground alpha image. This makes certain that the 3D objects will be hidden by Stonehenge. Now add your own 3D insect image—be creative in producing it. Adjust the position of the objects and the camera view so that all images appear in the window as shown.

STEP 6

We used LightWave®'s Sky Tracer plug-in to create a new sky for our image. Using this plug-in, we are able to create the desired sky background without having to worry about the resolution until we export the completed image.

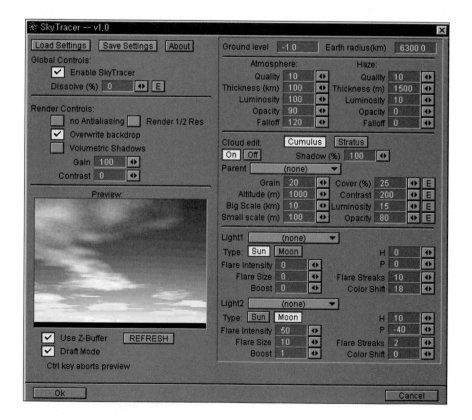

STEP 7

Now set the direction of the light for the insects as we did for the "Stonehenge" image so that they have shadows. Because radiosity mode wasn't supported by our 3D program, we used a weaker point light located opposite the main light. When your lighting is complete and your insects are arranged as you want them in the final image, render the image as a flat image file so that it can be edited in Photoshop.

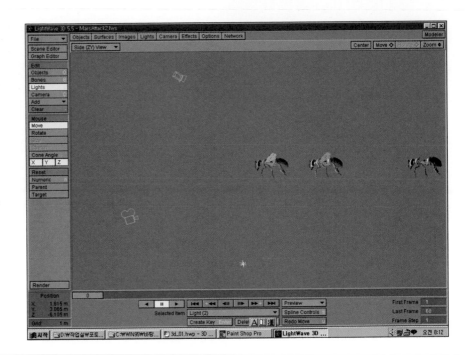

STEP 8

We now open the rendered image in Photoshop. To add a lifelike quality to the insects' wings, we'll apply the Motion Blur filter. First, because the angles of the left and right wings on the insects are different, make two copies of the image's "Background" layer and apply the Motion Blur filter to each, varying the Angle setting appropriately. Place the original layer at the top of the Layers palette and the two copies below it, first the layer for the left wings and then the layer for the right wings.

STEP 9

Select the original "Background" layer and choose Layer > Layer Mask > Reveal All. Setting the foreground color to black, use the Airbrush tool to paint over the insects' left wings on the mask. This allows the lower layers, with their blurred wings, to show through. After the left wings have been colored, choose Layer > Merge Down to combine the top two layers and then apply the same process to the insects' right wings.

STEP 10

To create depth, duplicate the "Background" layer again and apply the Gaussian Blur filter, then create a layer mask that eliminates the frontmost insects from the blurred layer.

STEP 11

To soften the image's colors slightly, choose Image > Adjustments > Variations and adjust the colors to your liking.

Project 13

Project 13 Source Files

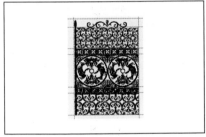

Gate

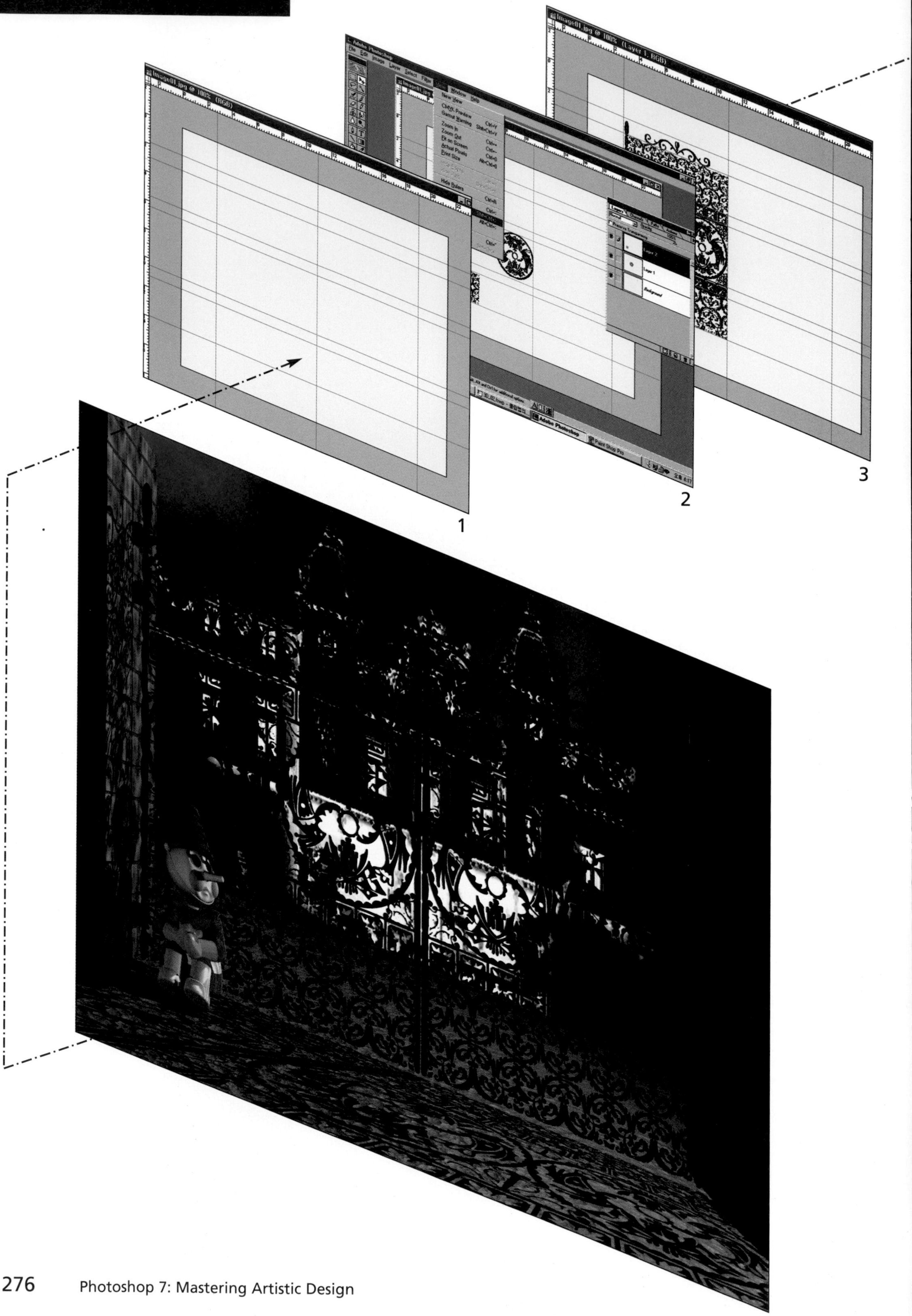
1
2
3

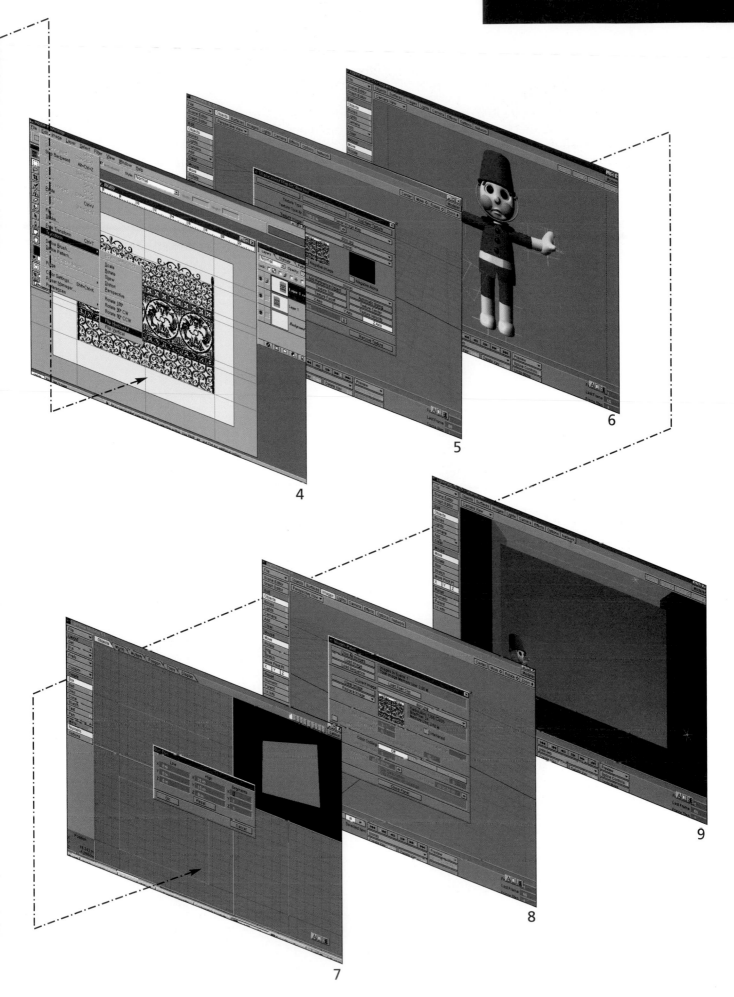

4

5

6

7

8

9

Introduction

Creating detailed and complex designs during 3D modeling is tedious, even for a professional. Fortunately, many techniques have been developed to simplify the creation of such complex designs, including the use of bump maps, displacement maps, and clip maps. Here, we will learn how to effectively utilize a clip map in LightWave 3D, a 3D modeling program from NewTek that has two interactive components: Layout and Modeler. A clip map is a black and white image that's used to hide portions of a 3D model from view; it can also block light so that it casts a shadow, as seen here.

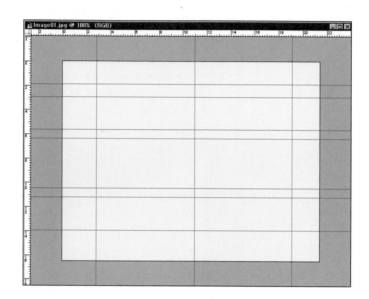

STEP 1

We will use Photoshop's Snap to Guide feature to create the clip map source image. Open a new file (choose File > New) and choose View > Show Rulers and then View > Show > Guides. Click a ruler and drag the mouse into the image to create a guide; place guides as shown to make a grid that you can use to build your image.

STEP 2

We used ornaments from Corel®'s MEGA GALLERY® art collection (to build an iron gate.) You can use any image elements you want to create a composite image that contains repeating elements, or you can use the "Gate" image included on the CD. (Open each image, adjust its size, and arrange it within the grid.) To simplify this process, first choose View > Snap To > Guides and View > Lock Guides. These options make the gate elements "stick" to the guide when you drag them into place.

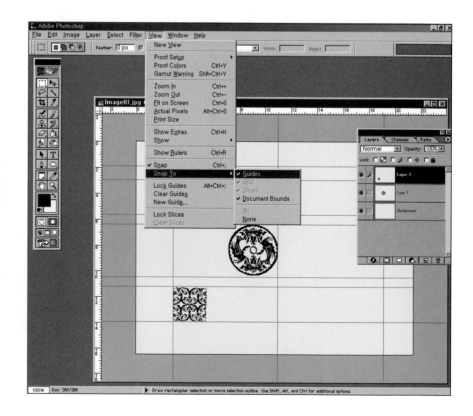

STEP 3

Copy elements as needed and position them using the guides. If the images you're using are the wrong size, choose Edit > Free Transform to adjust their sizes and shapes.

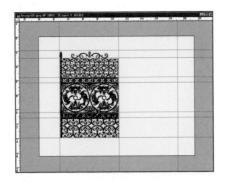

STEP 4

When one side of the design is complete, merge the layers, duplicate the resulting layer, and choose Edit > Transform > Flip Horizontal to create a symmetrical image. To use the completed image (in our case, an iron gate) as a clip map source, first convert it to grayscale mode and then save it in GIF format.

STEP 5

To build our composite image, we first opened the image we constructed in LightWave® Modeler and extruded a 3D object from it to create a three-dimensional iron gate. Then we switched to LightWave® Layout, which is used for building scenes from completed 3D elements. After clicking Appearance Options in the Objects panel, click the Clip Map button on the right. Selecting the Texture Image option shows the images added to the file in the previous step. Click an image and then click the Automatic Sizing button. This modifies the size of the selected image so that it fits with the object. Now set the Texture Axis option to Z-axis.

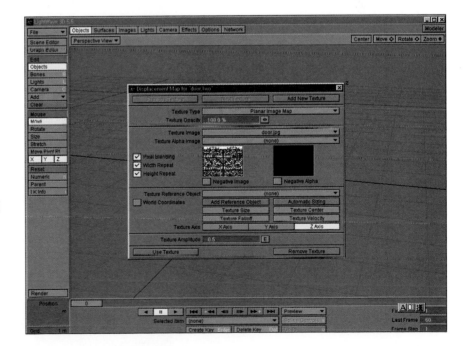

STEP 6

Click Load from Scene in the Objects panel to load a previously created 3D character. Using this feature, we will be able to load objects from different scenes in the current scene. The joints of our character, Little Soldier, were modeled individually using inverse kinematics (IK). IK allows us to pose the character as we please and is a fundamental technique for animation creation.

STEP 7

Now switch back to LightWave Modeler to apply the clip map to the iron gate. Choose Objects > Box Panel and create a flat window by pressing [shift]+X. The clip map allows us to create images in two dimensions, avoiding the unnecessary creation of many polygons, which would take up a lot of processing time.

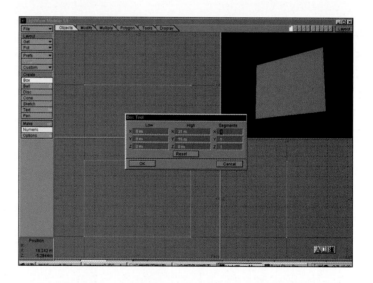

STEP 8

Back in Layout, click the Load Image button in the Images panel. When the dialog box opens, once again open the image created in Photoshop.

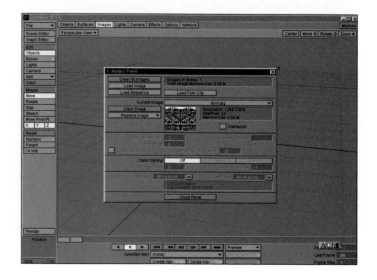

STEP 9

Finally, the image created using the clip map feature source is added to the scene and mapped to create the door. This makes the white portions of the gate transparent.

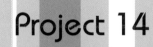

Project 14

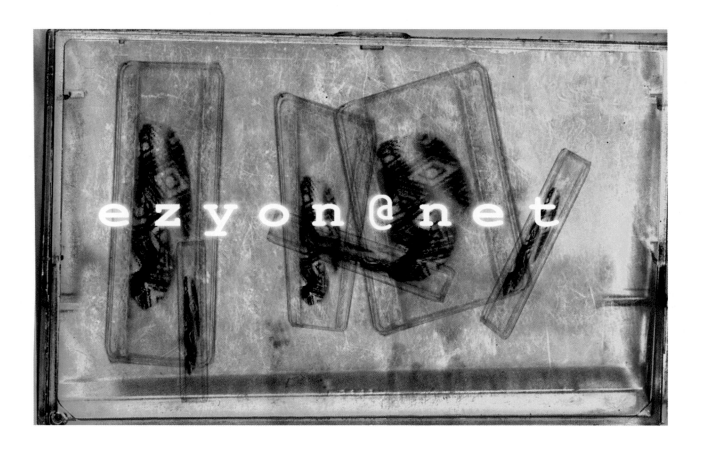

Project 14 Source Files

Scanned Image

Cassette Case

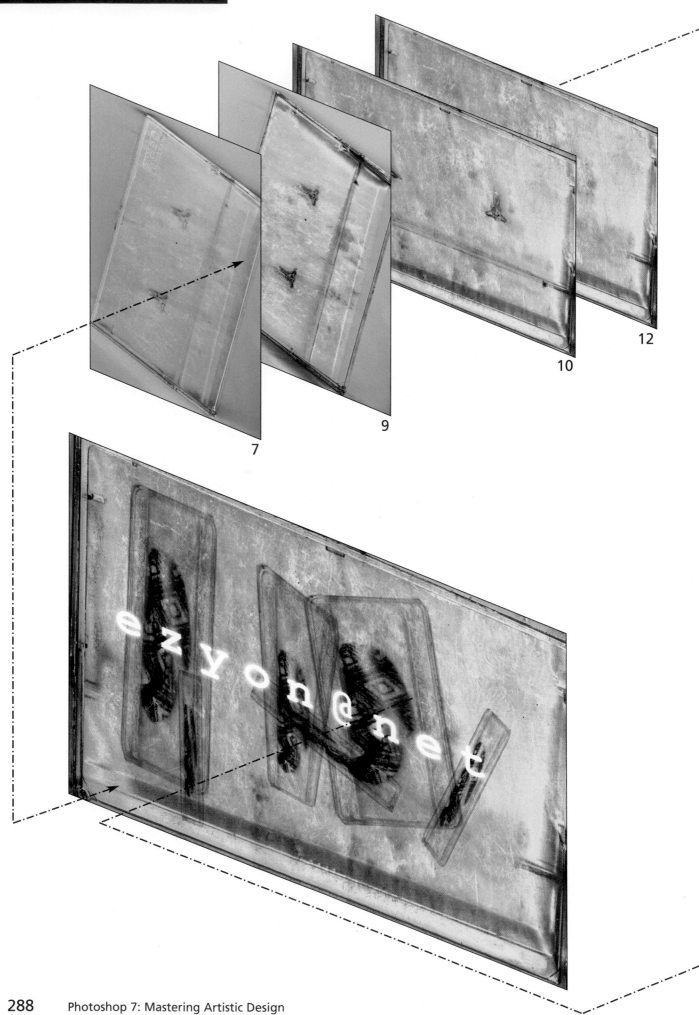

7

9

10

12

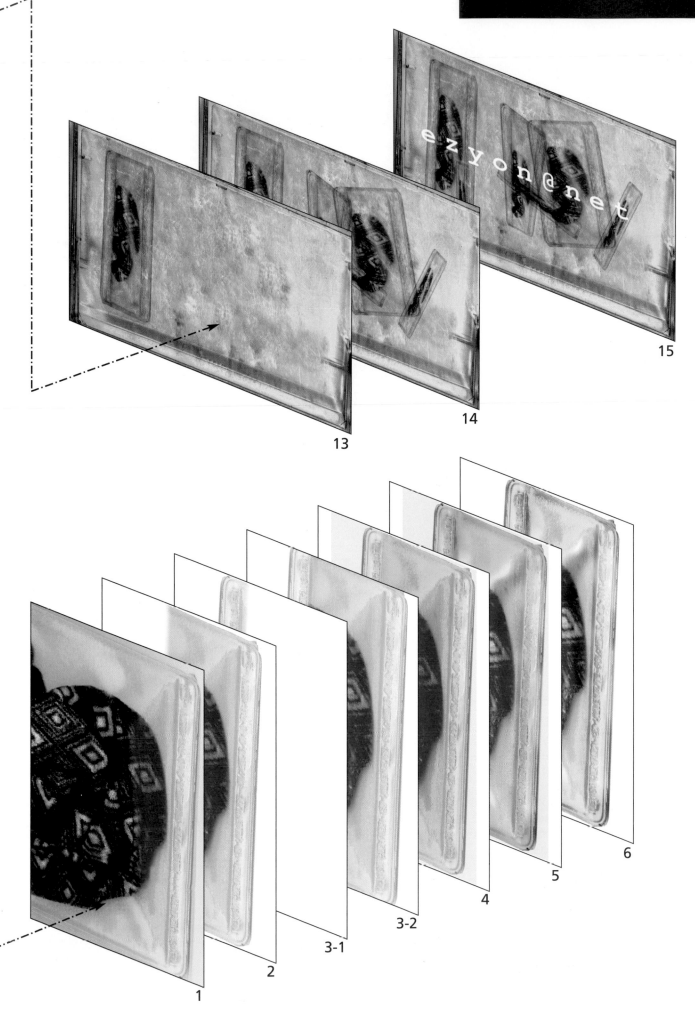

STEP 1

Open "Scanned Image"
(which shows a knit cap in
a plastic bag).

STEP 2

Switch to the Polygonal Lasso
tool (set the Feather value to 0
and check Anti-aliased), select
the outline of the image, and
copy it. Choose File > New to
open a new file and paste the
copied image. Name the new
layer "Plastic." (When a new
file is created in Photoshop, its
image size is automatically
adjusted to fit the image on
the clipboard.) We are going
to create a bag that is closed
on either end, so choose Image
> Canvas Size to add some
white space on the left side of
the image, and choose Edit >
Transform to rotate the image
as shown. Then switch to the
Polygonal Lasso tool again
(Feather value = 10; Anti-
aliased) to select the left edge
and press [del] to soften the
edge of the image.

STEP 3

Click on the "Plastic" layer and select the right side of the bag using the Polygonal Lasso tool (Feather value = 0; Anti-aliased). Choose Layer > New > Layer via Copy and name the new layer "Left Side." Choose Edit > Free Transform and place the layer such that it can be used to close the left edge of the bag. Because it needs to be connected to the image on the right, select the right edge of the "Left Side" layer using the Polygonal Lasso tool (Feather value = 10; Anti-aliased) and then press to soften the edge. Change the layer's blending mode to Multiply and its opacity to 100%.

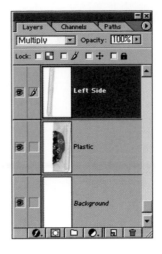

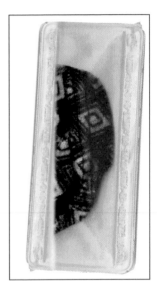

STEP 4

To beef up the edges of the plastic bag, copy and paste portions of the edge from the original source image file. Set the new layer's blending mode to Lighten and its opacity to 83% and name the layer "Add." Choose Edit > Free Transform to adjust the size and position of the image portions as in Step 3. To create softened edges, set the Feather value of the Lasso tool to 10 before selecting the bag edge sections.

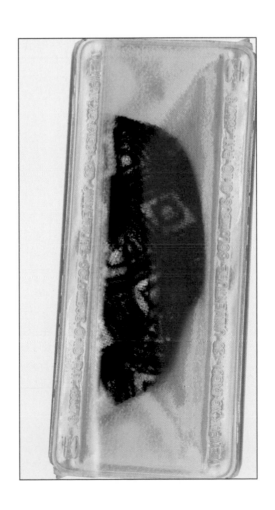

STEP 5

Choose Flatten Image from the Layers palette menu to merge the layers and then use the Clone Stamp tool to enhance the plastic quality of the empty portions of the bag. Switch to the Lasso tool (Feather value = 15) and select the lighter portions of the bag and then choose Image > Adjustments > Brightness/Contrast. Using this command to lighten or darken the areas will make it appear as if a folded cloth is inside the plastic with the cap. Finally, to emphasize the corners of the plastic, switch to the Burn tool and use it to darken portions of the edge with different brush sizes.

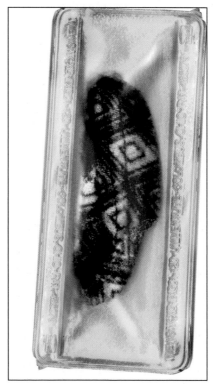

STEP 6

Choose Image > Mode > Grayscale to create a black and white image. One component of the final image is now complete.

STEP 7

Open the "Cassette Case" image.

STEP 8

We will now add color and a natural shadow to the image. In keeping with the cyber-theme of the title, "ezyon@net," we'll use fluorescent color. Choose Image > Adjustments > Brightness/Contrast and make the Brightness setting 0 and the Contrast setting +61. This gives strong contrast to the image. Next, choose Image > Adjustments, Hue/Saturation.

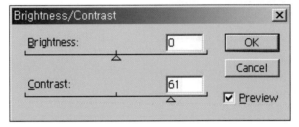

STEP 9

Adjust the Hue slider to -103 and the Saturation slider to +14. This adds a yellow-green fluorescence to the cassette holder. In the next steps, we will remove the unnecessary details from the center of the image.

STEP 10

Choose Edit > Free Transform
to resize and rotate the image
so that the case is horizontal.
Then, select the portion of the
cassette case that will be used
for the background using the
Polygonal Lasso tool (Feather
value = 0; Anti-aliased). Choose
Image > Crop to isolate the
portion of the case that we're
going to use.

STEP 11

Re-open the black and white image you created in Steps 1 through 6.

STEP 12

Now all we have to do is
remove the spindle pegs and
mold lines from the center of
the image. To do this, use the
Clone Stamp tool to copy
blank areas of the image or
use the Lasso tool (Feather
value = 20; Anti-aliased) to
copy and paste blank portions
of the image over the pegs
and lines.

STEP 13

Copy the grayscale image and
paste it into the color image.
Don't worry about the white
edges—they'll be hidden by
this new layer's blending
mode. Choose Edit > Free
Transform and adjust the size
and position of the plastic bag
layer, then set its blending
mode to Multiply and its opacity to 100%.

STEP 14

Make several copies of the plastic bag layer and place them
as shown here. (The blending mode and opacity are kept at
Multiply and 100%, respectively, for all these layers.)

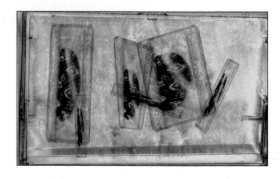

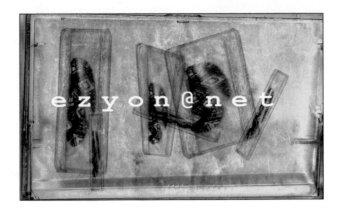

STEP 15

After adjusting the font size and spacing and setting the Foreground color to white, type in the text "ezyon@net" as shown here. Make sure the type layer is at the top of the Layers palette.

STEP 16

Name the text layer "Text Original," then make a copy of this layer and name it "Text Copy." Choose Layer > Rasterize > Type and then make sure that the Preserve Transparency box at the top of the Layers palette is unchecked for this layer. Choose Filter > Other > Minimum and set the Radius to 2 pixels.

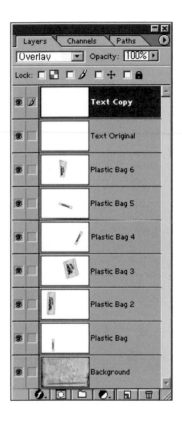

STEP 17

Choose Filter > Blur > Gaussian Blur and set the Radius value to 4.4. Try a few different blending modes for this layer; we set its blending mode to Overlay and its opacity to 100%.

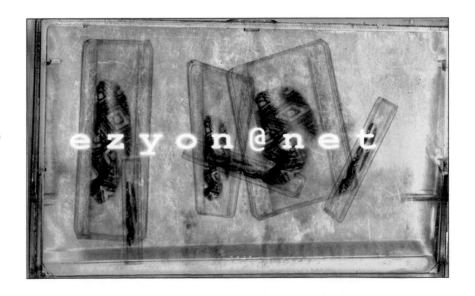

Project 15

Project 15 Source Files

Sketch

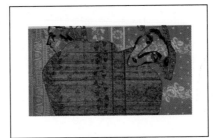

Modified Sketch

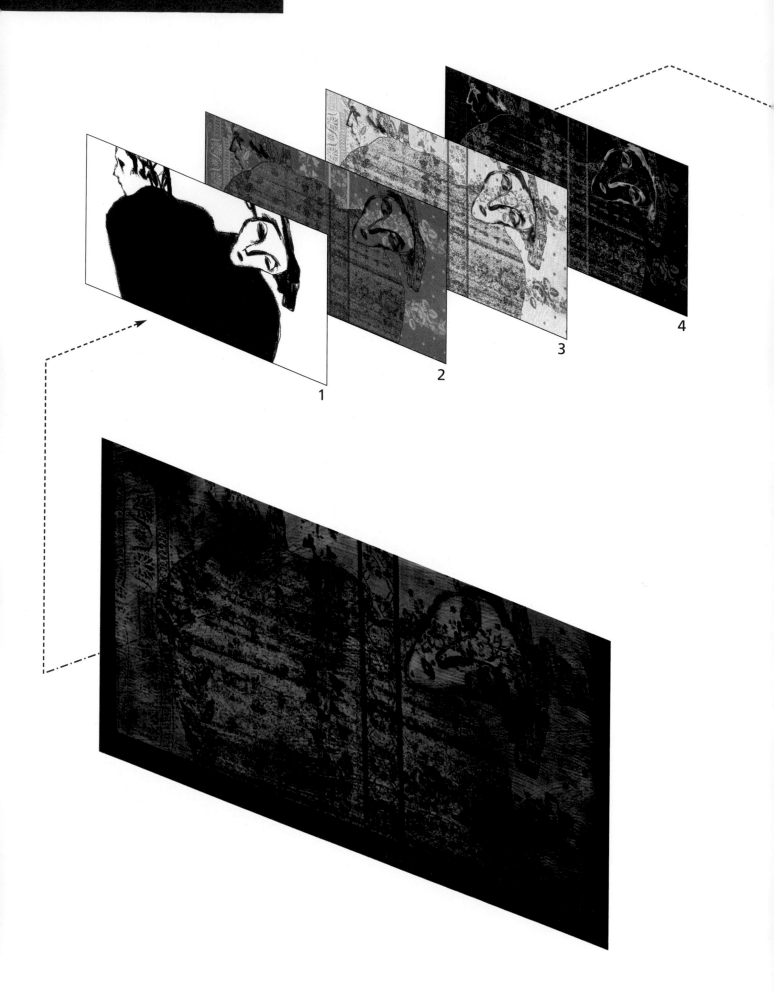

1

2

3

4

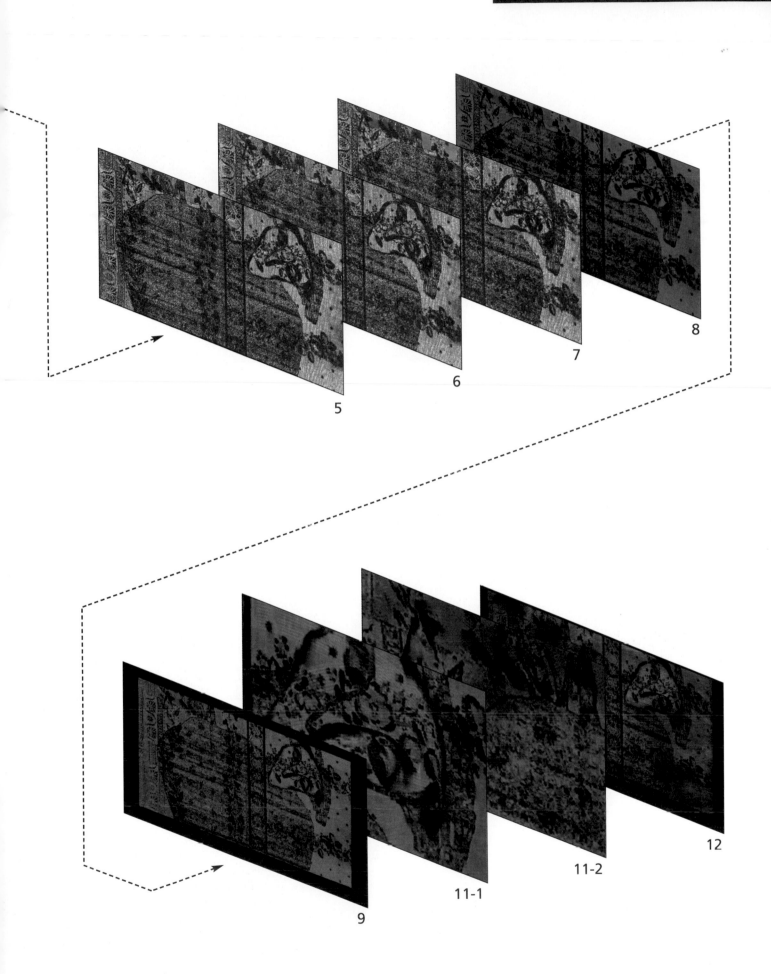

STEP 1

We started this project by sketching a bundled shape with two heads that face opposite directions (the "Sketch" image file). Then we drew this image in a brown tone using Procreate Painter®.

STEP 2

After adding several textures to create the desired form, we chose Image > Mode > Duotone and converted the image to a quadtone to add the desired colors. We then converted the image to RGB color mode and used Color Balance to modify the color. To make the image come alive, a cream color was added. (If you want to start from this point, open the image file "Modified Sketch" and convert it to RGB color mode.) From this point, open the image in Photoshop, select it (using Select All), and copy and paste it into a new image. Set the new layer's blending mode to Exclusion and its opacity to 100%. To add the roughened interior texture, select the black portion using the Magic Wand tool and choose Filter > Noise > Add Noise.

STEP 3

Convert the image to grayscale mode and duplicate the layer, setting the new layer's blending mode to Difference and its opacity to 100%.

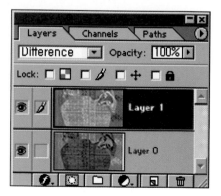

STEP 4

Choose Flatten Image from the Layers palette menu and use the Crop tool to cut out the desired portion of the image.

STEP 5

Choose Image > Adjustments > Invert.

STEP 6

Now, choose Image > Adjustments > Levels (you can select part of the image before using Levels if you prefer).

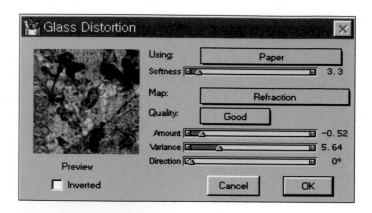

STEP 7

Save the image and open the file in Procreate Painter®. Apply the Glass Distortion filter. (If you don't have Procreate Painter®, you can achieve a similar effect in Photoshop by choosing Filter > Noise > Median.)

STEP 8

As we can see, some areas stand out from the rest of the image. We retouched these areas in Procreate Painter® using the Brush tool. Choose Water > Just Add Water from the Brushes palette and rub the brush over the selected areas. The Smudge (Fingertip) tool would distort the image, but the Just Add Water tool creates the effect of a blotted image. If you don't have Painter, try using Photoshop's Smart Blur feature to achieve a similar effect.

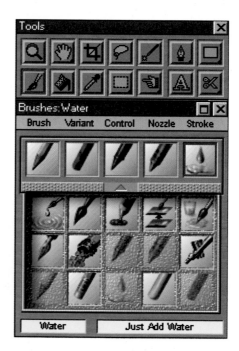

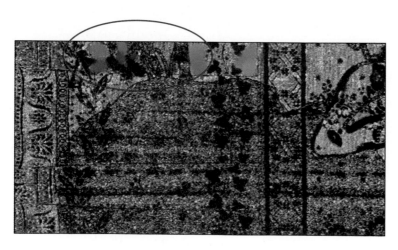

STEP 9

Open the image in Photoshop again and use both Levels and Brightness/Contrast to adjust the image's tones as shown.

STEP 10

Setting the background color to black, enlarge the canvas size from the Image menu to create a black frame around the image as shown here.

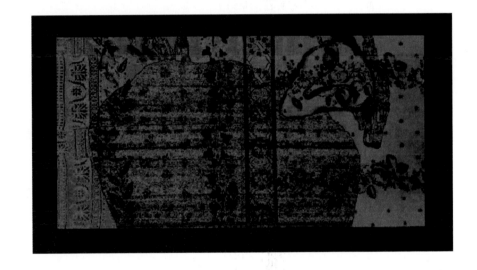

STEP 11

Let's now open this image in Procreate Painter® again to add texture. Selecting the area to be modified, choose Select > Float to convert the image to a floater and list it in the Floater List in the Objects palette. (The concept of Procreate Painter®'s floater is similar to Photoshop's layer.) After selecting, set the floater's composite method (similar to blending mode in Photoshop) to Gel mode in the Controls palette.

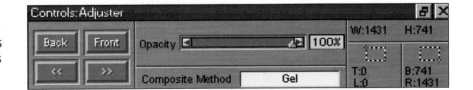

STEP 12

Now we'll add some rough sawtooth scratches to the image. Click in the blank area at the bottom of the Floater List to deactivate the floater, then choose Pens > Scratchboard Rake from the Brushes palette. Adjust the brush's size and opacity in the Controls palette and set the Foreground color to white. (Use the scratchboard rake brush to create faint lines in the image as shown.) When you're done, click on "Floater 1" in the Floater List and click the Drop button to merge the floater back into the main image. Save and close the file.

STEP 13

Open the scratched image in Photoshop again to add finishing touches. Using the Crop tool, trim the image as shown. Use the Burn tool to create artificially burned areas in the image, adjusting the thickness and intensity of the Brush tool to vary the burns.

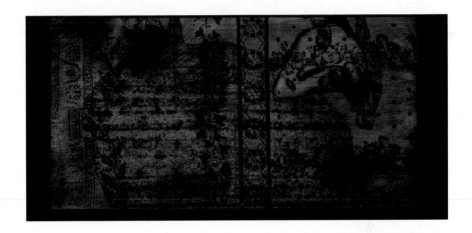

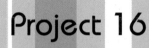

Project 16

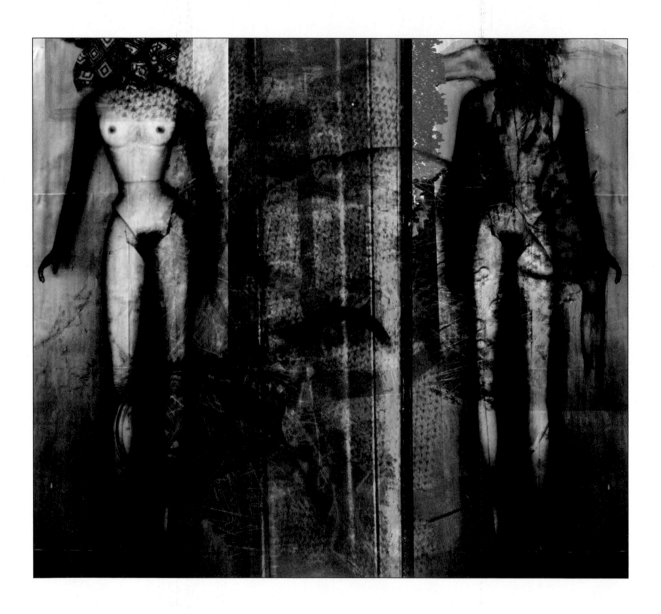

Project 16 Source Files

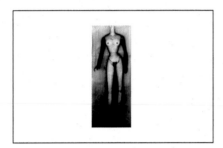

Doll

Source 1

Source 2

Source 3

Source 4

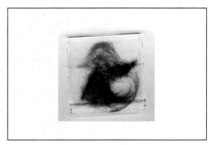

Source 5

Source 6

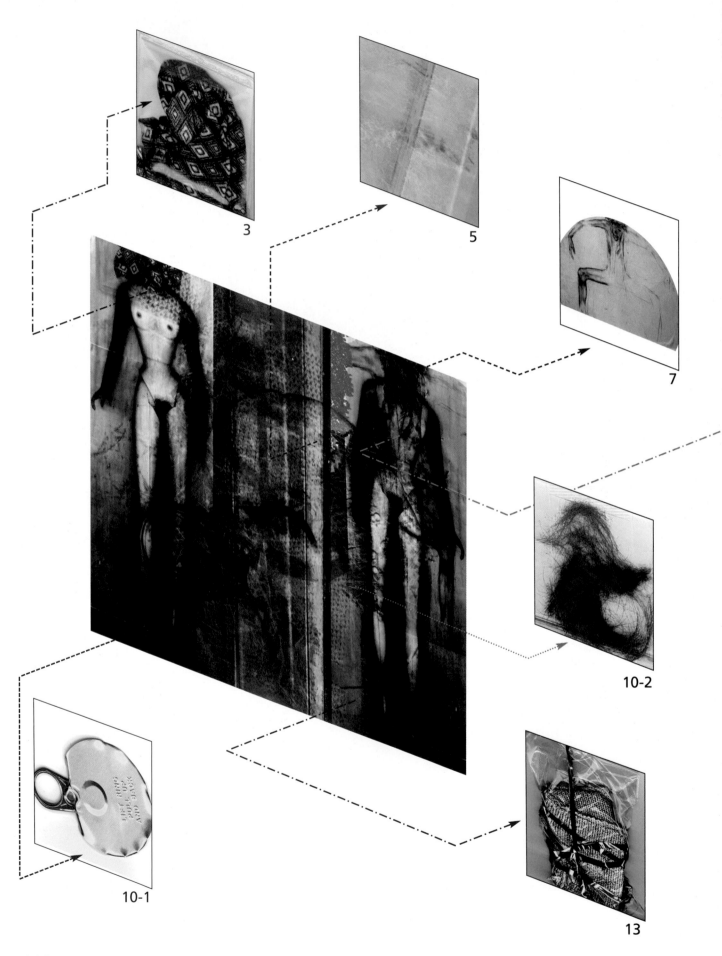

3

5

7

10-2

10-1

13

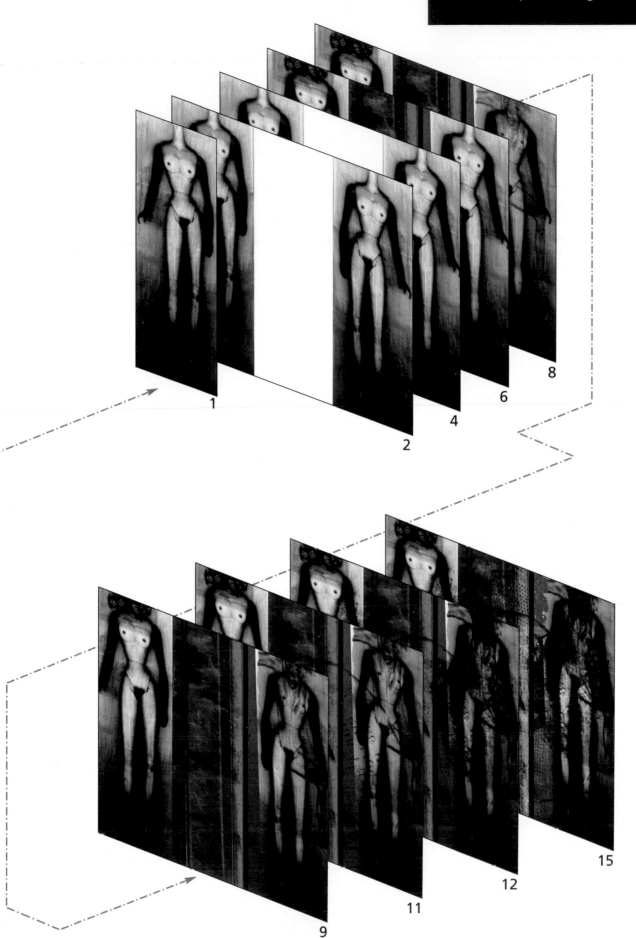

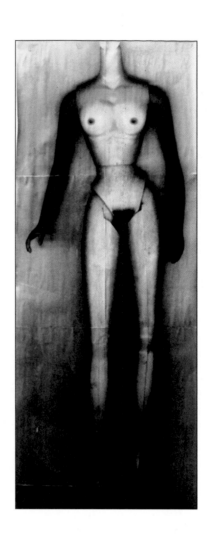

STEP 1

This first step is somewhat complex. First, we scanned the body of a doll. Then we used the Airbrush and Clone tools to draw in additional parts. Next, we used various image adjustment commands to modify the image's color. Finally, we printed the image and modified the print-out manually, then photographed the modified image and scanned the resulting print. The result of all these steps is contained in the image file "Doll."

STEP 2

Open the "Doll" image file, triple the width to the right using canvas size, and place a copy of the doll image on right side of the canvas as shown.

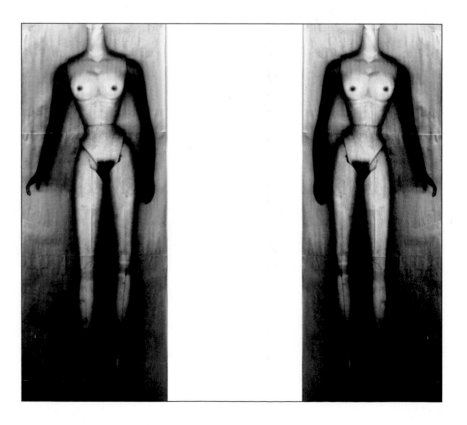

STEP 3

Open the "Source 1" image file (a scan of cloth in a plastic bag); we'll place this image on the shoulders of the doll on the left.

STEP 4

Select all of the "Source 1" image, copy it, and paste it into the composite image. Press [ctrl]+[d] and use Free Transform to proportionally adjust the size of the cloth image and position it as shown here. Set the new layer's blending mode to Multiply and its opacity to 100% and name it "Head." Then use Color Balance and Hue/Saturation to adjust the color.

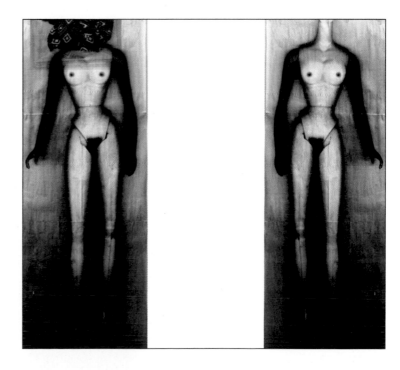

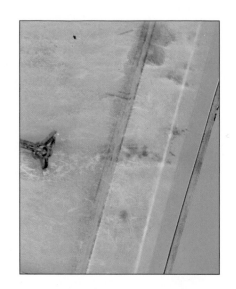

STEP 5

Open the "Source 2" image, which we'll place in the center of the composite.

STEP 6

Drag the "Source 2" image into the blank space in the center of the composite image. Keeping the new layer's blending mode at Normal and its opacity at 100%, name the layer "Barrier." Use Free Transform to rotate the image so that its lines are straight, then use the Marquee tool to select and delete the portions of the layer that overlap the doll images. We are going to fill in this middle area with a dark color that stands out from the rest of the image. Choose Image > Adjustments > Brightness/Contrast to darken the layer's color and create a strong contrast. Then choose Image > Adjustments > Hue/Saturation and use the sliders to lower the saturation and to slightly alter the hue so that it will blend with the images that will be put into place later on.

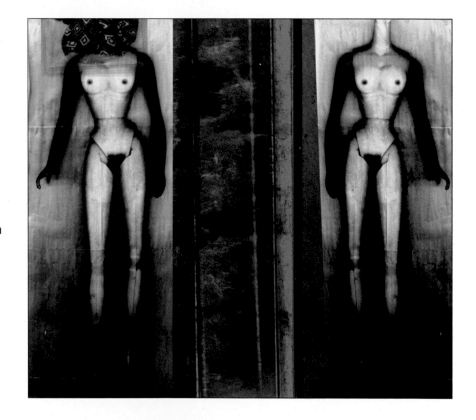

STEP 7

Now open the "Source 3" image file, a scanned photo of a pencil sketch.

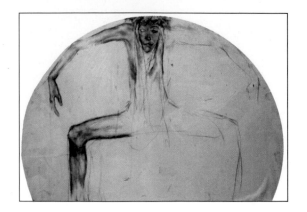

STEP 8

This image will overlay the doll on the right. Selecting the white background of "Source 3," invert it and then copy the selection. Paste the sketch into the composite image. Again, use Free Transform to adjust the image's size appropriately and flip it over. Use the Lasso tool to select and cut out the left leg of the sketched figure, and then use Free Transform to flip the leg over and move to the right side of the figure as shown. Set the layer's blending mode to Multiply and its opacity to 90%; name the layer "Shoulder." The base image for this project is almost complete.

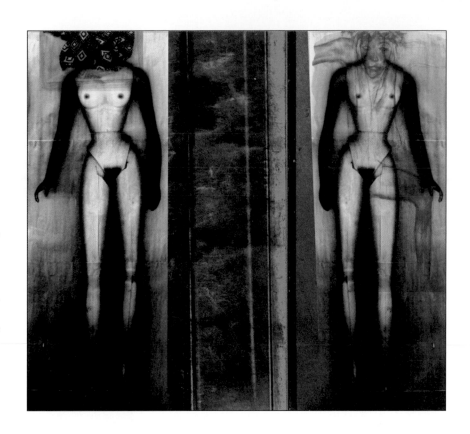

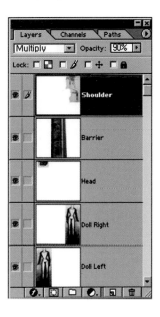

STEP 9

Choose Flatten Image from the Layers palette menu. To modify the image's color, press [ctrl]+[b] or choose Image > Adjustments > Color Balance. Then use the sliders to adjust the yellow, green, and red tones so that the image appears slightly faded and darker.

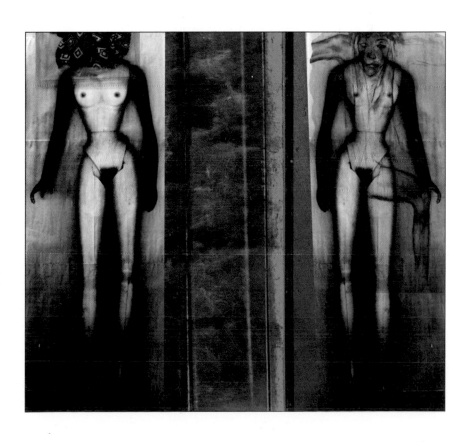

STEP 10

In the next steps, we'll add a can pop top image and use scanned hair to add texture to the composite image. To create the scanned image, hair was placed inside a plastic case and scanned

STEP 11

Open the "Source 4" image. Choose Select > Color Range and select the white area around the can top (use a Fuzziness value of 48), then click OK. Invert the selection. Choose Select > Feather and apply a Feather value of 3 to the selection, then copy and paste into the composite image. Name the new layer "Can." After setting the layer's blending mode to Multiply and its opacity to 100%, size and position the image as shown.

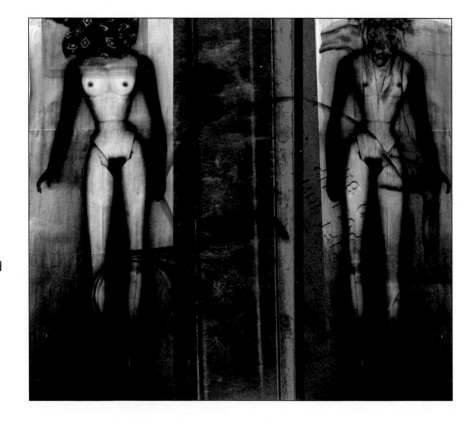

STEP 12

Open the "Source 5" image and use Color Range to select the red portions of the image (set the Fuzziness value to 100). Choose Select > Modify > Expand and set the value to 4. Now, copy and paste into the composite image. After setting the blending mode to Multiply and the opacity to 100%, name this layer "Hair." Because we want to arrange the hair on both dolls, use the Lasso tool to select the left half of the hair. Then choose Layer > New > Layer via Cut. This turns the "Hair" layer into two layers. Use Free Transform to arrange the two halves on either side of the image as shown. The blending mode and opacity of the two new layers remain Multiply and 100%, respectively. Name the layers "Hair Left" and "Hair Right" and drag them below the "Can" layer in the Layers palette.

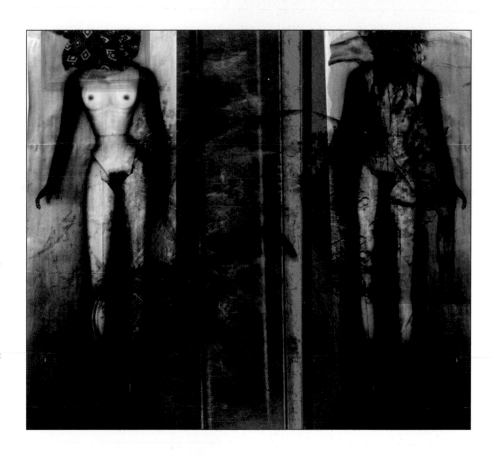

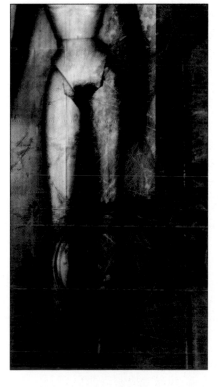

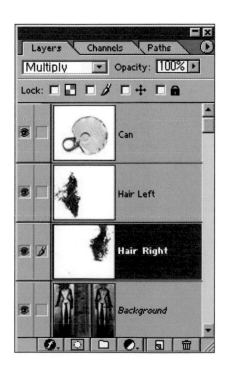

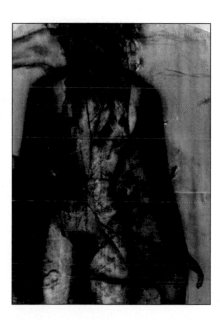

STEP 13

Open the "Source 6" image file. Switch to the Lasso tool and set the Feather value to 5 in the Options bar. Use the Lasso tool to select the portion of the image that we want to use and then copy and paste it into the composite file. Use Free Transform to center this image and then set the layer's blending mode to Overlay and its opacity to 40%. Name the layer "Texture." Observe the contrast between light and dark.

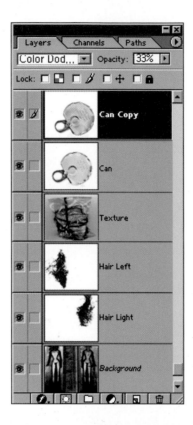

STEP 14

In the Layers palette, click the "Can" layer and click the Duplicate Layer button to create "Can Copy."

STEP 15

Choose Image > Adjustments > Hue/ Saturation and drop the Saturation value to 0 to make the layer grayscale. Change the layer's blending mode to Color Dodge and its opacity to 33%, then move the image slightly to the right. To cover the white area to the left of the right-hand doll, switch to the Magic Wand tool and click on the "Background" layer. Set the tool's Tolerance value to 10 in the Options bar and click on a yellow area of the background. Use Free Transform to shift the selected pixels into place as shown.

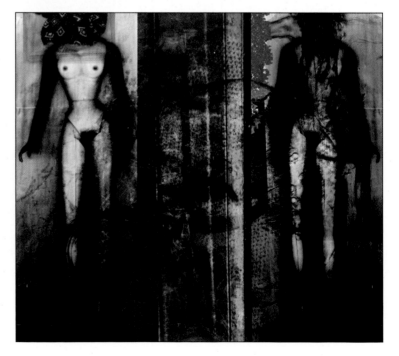

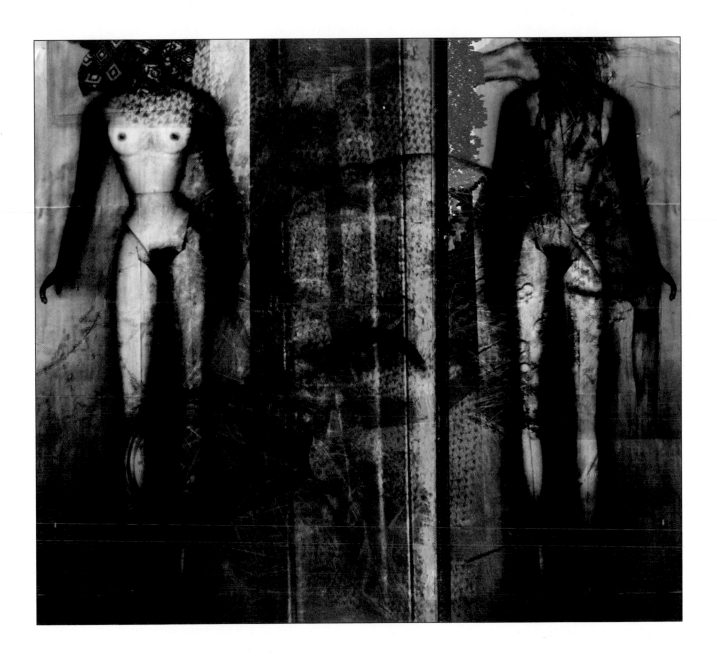

Photoshop 7: Mastering Artistic Design

Project 17

Project 17 Source Files

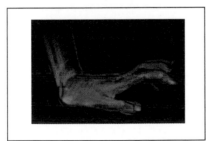

Sketch

Source 1

Shrivel Center

Source 2-1

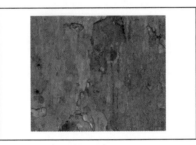

Source 2-2

Source 2-3

Source 4

Hand

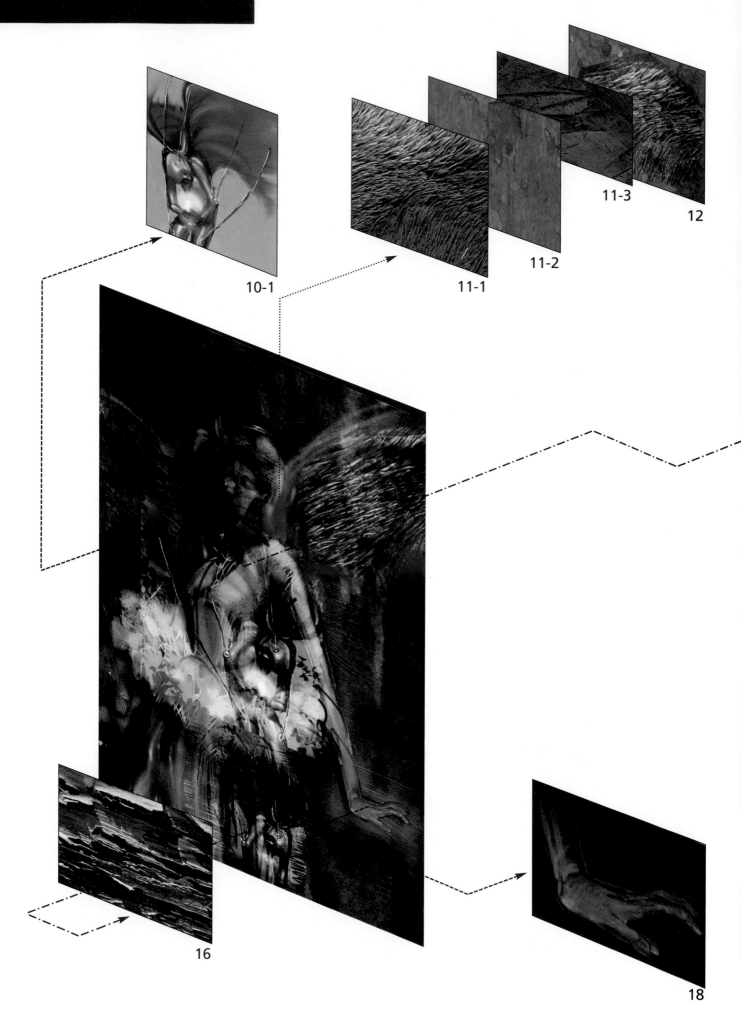

10-1

11-1

11-2

11-3

12

16

18

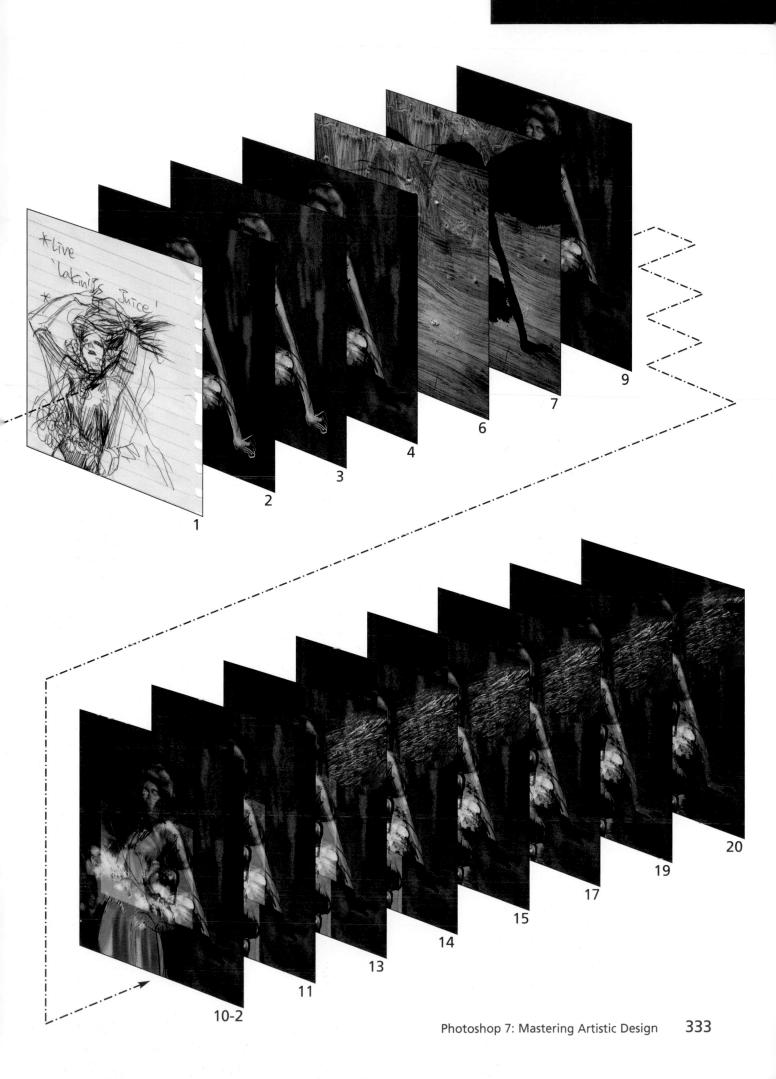

Introduction

I created this sketch while in a bar. I combined the sketch with another source image, a sudden brainstorm that I had while working on another project. A variety of textures were applied to these images to develop a story with the theme of shriveling and unfolding.

STEP 1

It's good to get into the habit of making sketches of those sudden inspirations. You never know when they will come in handy. The rough sketch that I scribbled haphazardly in my pocket notebook forms the basis for this project.

STEP 2

I redrew the sketch in Procreate Painter® using the Brush tool and the Color Overlay command to add color and texture to the image at the same time. I used both large and small Pastel brushes to color the sketch. The image was completed in no time.

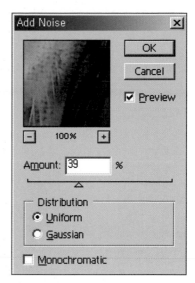

STEP 3

After opening the "Sketch" image file in Photoshop, make sure that it is in RGB color mode (all the images used in this project should be RGB). Switch to the Lasso tool and select the background, then adjust the Feather value to 10. Choose Filter > Noise > Add Noise, click Uniform, and set the Amount value to 39.

STEP 4

Choose Filter > Artistic > Palette Knife. This completes the basic background. I didn't particularly care for the hand, so I erased it with the idea of drawing in a new one later.

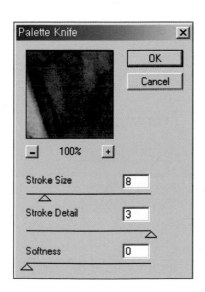

STEP 5

Now we'll add texture to the background. Open the "Source 1" image file and choose Image > Mode > Grayscale. Choose Image > Rotate Canvas > 90° CW to match the orientation of the sketch image.

STEP 6

Choose Image > Adjustments > Brightness/ Contrast to increase the texture's contrast. Select the completed texture and copy it. Then, create a new channel in the composite image and paste the texture image into it. Using Free Transform, adjust the size of the texture to fit.

STEP 7

Activate the "Background" layer and select the outline of the woman again using the Lasso tool (Feather: 0; Anti-aliased), then fill in the selection with black. Copy the entire channel and paste it into a new document window. (Choose File > New to create a new document.) Then choose File > Save As to save this file in native Photoshop format.

STEP 8

Return to the composite image and choose Filter > Texture > Texturizer.

STEP 9

In the Texturizer dialog box, choose Load Texture from the Texture pop-up menu and locate the channel image file you created in Step 7. Set the Relief value to 20 and the Light Direction to Top Right. Because this texture will be used as the map, leave the Scaling value at 100%—the same as the image. Click OK; a roughened, black and white texture appears in the image background.

STEP 10

Open the "Shrivel Center" image file, copy it, and paste it into the composite image. Then use Free Transform to adjust the size of the image. Set the new layer's blending mode to Hard Light and its opacity to 85% and name it "Shrivel Center."

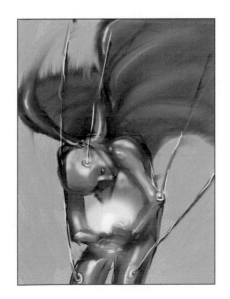

STEP 11

Paste two additional copies of the "Shrivel Center" image into the composite image and then use Free Transform to adjust their size and position. Name the top layer "Shrivel Top" and set its blending mode to Difference and its opacity to 33%. For the bottom layer, set the blending mode to Hard Light and the opacity to 90% and name it "Shrivel Bottom." Because the outline is too dark, we will slowly remove portions of it as we work.

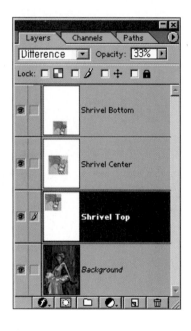

STEP 12

To expand the image in the center, we decided to add wings using texture. Open the "Source 2-1" image file. Switch to the Lasso tool and set its Feather value to 10 in the Options bar. Select the center of the hair pattern, copy it, and paste it into the "Source 2-2" image file. Set the new layer's blending mode to Overlay and its opacity to 100%. The bone structure for the wings will come from the "Source 2-3" image file. Select the center of the image using the Polygon Lasso tool and copy and paste the selection over the hair portion of the wing. Set the new layer's blending mode to Multiply and its opacity to 100%.

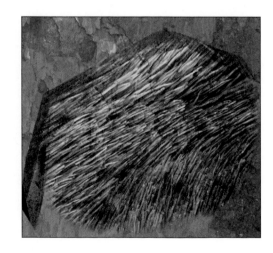

STEP 13

Combine the three layers of Step 12 by choosing Flatten Image from the Layers palette. Switch to the Lasso tool and set its Feather value to 8, then use it to select and copy the wing and paste it into the composite image. Setting the new layer's blending mode to Hard Light and the opacity to 100%, use Free Transform to adjust the wing's size and position. Use this same process to add the left wing. Set the blending mode of the left wing to Overlay and its opacity to 90%.

STEP 14

Now we will fine-tune the images that we loaded one at a time. From the images pasted in Steps 10 and 11, we start with the centermost image. Selecting "Shrivel Center," choose Layer > Add Layer Mask and select the portion of the mask to remove using the Lasso tool. Then, after setting the Background color to black, press the key to fill the selected area with black and hide that portion of the image with the layer mask. The result should look like the image here.

STEP 15

Retouch the "Shrivel Bottom" layer in the same way.

STEP 16

In order to modify the "Shrivel Top" layer, we will use the prepared image.

STEP 17

Create a new channel and paste the contents of the "Source 4" image into it. Use Free Transform to adjust the size and position of the image so that it fits in the same space as the "Shrivel Top" layer. Name the channel "Noise." After selecting the "Shrivel Top" layer, choose Select > Load Selection to create a selection from the "Noise" channel. Choose Layer > Add Layer Mask > Reveal All and make black the Foreground color and use the Airbrush tool to fill portions of the selection with black on the layer mask. Because the vertical pattern in itself is inadequate, select the white portions of the "Noise" channel and use Free Transform to reduce the pattern and rotate it 90 degrees. Then use the Airbrush tool again to mask portions of the image until you arrive at the desired effect.

STEP 18

Now, in order to add the hand, we need to create a hand image. Using your own hand as a guide, use Painter's Pastel Brush tool to draw a hand and finish it with the Pencil Brush tool. Or, if you prefer, use my hand image ("Hand").

STEP 19

Open the "Hand" image in Photoshop. After carefully selecting the hand using the Lasso tool (Feather: 0; Anti-aliased), copy and paste the selection into the composite image. Use Free Transform to adjust the size and position. Then, setting the Foreground color to a medium skin tone, fill in the hand using the Airbrush tool. We then slightly retouched the left hand as well. Keeping the new layer's blending mode at Normal and its opacity at 100%, name the layer "Hand."

STEP 20

We will now draw using the Brush tool. Drawing directly on the background will create big problems later on if we should make a mistake, so create a new layer and place it at the very top of the Layers palette. Use the Airbrush tool to hide the backbone of the wing and draw in the lower part of the wing, using a natural color. We added detail on the lower left part of the dress as well.

STEP 21

To modify the image's color, create another new layer. Use the Fill command to completely fill the layer using any color—this prevents the alert dialog telling us that a filter cannot be applied to a transparent layer. Set the Background color to beige and the Foreground color to green and choose Filter > Render > Clouds. Press [ctrl]+[f] to reapply the filter and create a more complex cloud effect. Set the layer's blending mode to Overlay and its opacity to 90%. Then use the Airbrush tool to add finishing touches directly on the layer.

Working with Other Graphic Tools

Introduction

This chapter contains a brief summary and overview of the different programs that were used along with Photoshop to create the many images that appear throughout this book. You may recall that in many portions of the book, rather than an in-depth explanation, we simply stated, "Refer to 'Working with Other Graphic Tools' in the back of this book." Here is where we will offer a more detailed look at our methods of working with these other graphics programs. Learning to use new programs to create images can be complex and difficult. However, as we all know, it is very difficult to obtain a full range of effects using just one program. This skill of learning to use various programs efficiently as the situation calls for them is very useful. Relying on only the tools offered by a certain program greatly diminishes one's creativity. With that said, let's now learn about those other graphic tools.

POSER + PAINTER
Project 1: Creating the face
Project 6: Creating the body

BRYCE
Project 2: Rendering the figure
Project 7: Creating the UFO

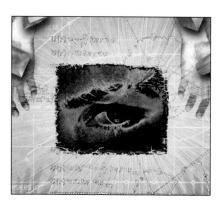

PAINTER'S FINISHING TEXTURE EFFECT
Texture Effect 1
Texture Effect 2

Poser + Painter

The interfaces of these two programs are similarly and logically organized, so that even the beginner can use them with ease. The famous Procreate Painter program includes traditional art tools that can be used within the computer. Curious Labs Poser is a 3D modeling program that can be used to add a wide variety of poses and motion to bodies and also includes an animation feature. Our project used Poser to model a cold, mechanical image that was retouched using Painter to create a more artistic and natural picture. The use of these two programs to create the image is explained very briefly here.

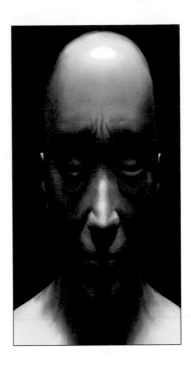

Project 1: Creating the face

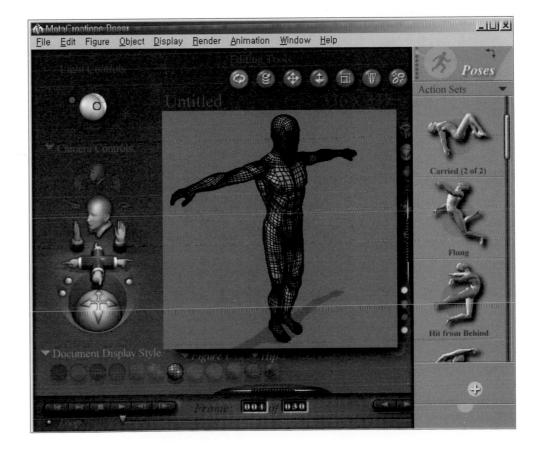

STEP 1
Starting up Poser reveals the interface shown above.

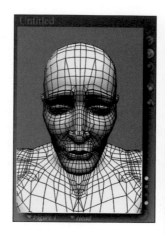

STEP 2

We chose the FaceCam to render the face and clicked the Z Translate button so that only the face appeared enlarged in the window.

STEP 3

We chose Render > Render Options and specified the image resolution.

STEP 4

This is the rendered image opened in a new window.

STEP 5

This new rendered image could be saved in TIFF or BMP format using the Save As command. We saved this file in the more commonly used TIFF format.

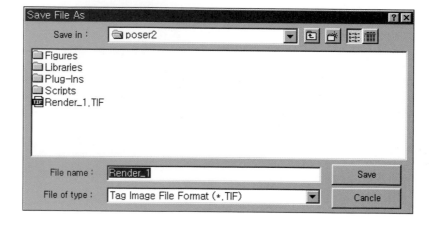

STEP 6
Then we started up Painter.

STEP 7
We opened the rendered image file.

 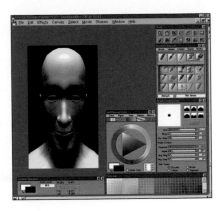

STEP 8
In the Art Materials palette, we opened the Paper "drawer" and chose Basic. Then, in the Brushes palette, we open the Brush drawer to display the choices. For this project, we mostly used the Fine Brush.

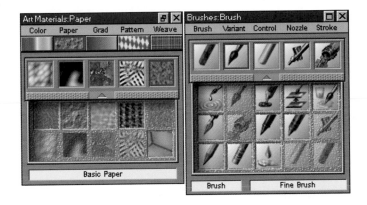

STEP 9
Because the face appeared too stiff, we used the Brush tool to draw in the desired expression. We specified the paint color by pressing the key to turn the cursor into an eyedropper and then clicking on the existing skin of the face.

STEP 10
We completed the image by using the Airbrush tool to soften portions of the image where the brush strokes were too rough.

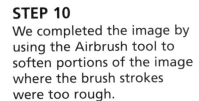 

Project 6: Creating the Body

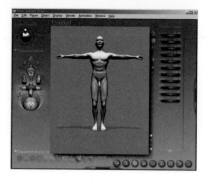

STEP 1
We started up Poser.

STEP 2
We then created the desired pose. We could also use any one of the poses that are saved in the program's library. We used the Translate, Twist, Rotate, and Z-translate tools from the Pose controls to create the pose.

STEP 3
We rendered the image and then saved it as an image file.

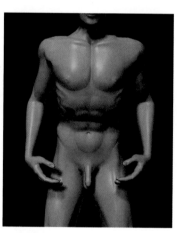

STEP 4
To select only the torso, we used the Crop tool from Photoshop to remove the head and legs from the rest of the body.

STEP 5
We then saved the image with a different name and opened it in Painter. There we retouched the borders of the image to roughen them. We specified a Paper option and used the Charcoal brush to add an overall soft, yet strong crumpled effect. We applied this effect using varying sizes of the Brush tool. Then, we saved the image and opened it in Photoshop to blend it with the background.

BRYCE

Bryce is a program from Corel that is used to create naturalistic 3D models. This program can be used to create mountainous and flat terrain, as well as rendering natural cloud, star, and moon shapes. In this case, we wanted to create metallic shapes that reflected a sky. Let's take a closer look at the creation of the image used in Project 2.

Project 2: Rendering the Figure

STEP 1

First, we started up Bryce.

STEP 2

We chose one of the figures displayed in the Create toolbar.

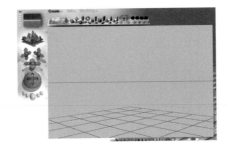

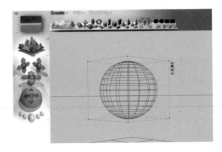

STEP 3

Selecting the figure and clicking the Edit menu displayed a Materials dialog box that we used to add texture to the object.

STEP 4

We chose Mirror from the Simple&Fast category of textures.

STEP 5

The background sky is added in the Sky&Fog dialog box. Here we chose "A cold wind blowing."

STEP 6

We clicked the Rendering Preview button from the top left to check the view of the sky, the camera angle, and the position of the figure. Then we rendered the completed image.

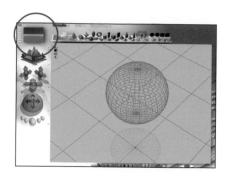

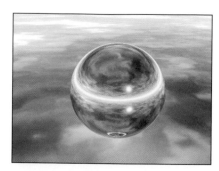

STEP 7

Choosing the Render To Disk command displays a dialog box asking for the resolution of the rendered image. We entered the appropriate resolution and saved the file in TIFF format.

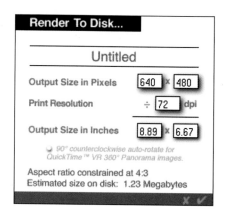

STEP 8

When we opened the image in Photoshop, we selected the outline of the figure and inverted the selection so we could remove the sky background. This completed the first image. The process for creating the other figures was the same.

Project 7: Creating the UFO

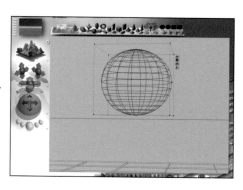

STEP 1

The process here was the same as that for creating the figure above. The only difference is that the UFO was created by specifying different camera angles for the same circular object. First, we created a spherical object.

STEP 2

Then we added the flattened sphere from the Create toolbar.

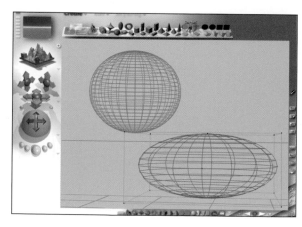

STEP 3

We arranged the two objects so that the sphere was situated directly in the middle of the flattened sphere.

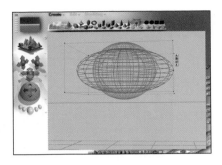

STEP 4

We selected the flattened sphere and copied and pasted it. Then, we adjusted the size of the second flat sphere so that it was even flatter.

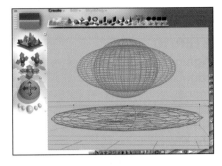

STEP 5

We selected the spheres created in Steps 1 and 2 and grouped them to keep the two objects.

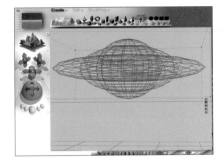

STEP 6

Next we grouped the sphere created in Step 4 with the two spheres grouped in Step 5.

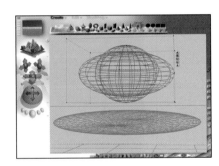

STEP 7

In the Create toolbar, we clicked on the sphere again to add another sphere to the image, then placed it at the bottom of the window.

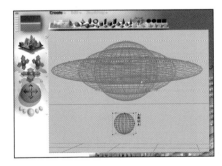

STEP 8

We copied and pasted the small sphere five times to create the image seen here.

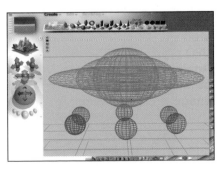

The majority of these textures was created using Paper and Charcoal. This is the same process that was used to create the torso for Project 6 explained earlier. The quality of the texture varies widely depending on the type of paper used and the many Surface Control functions in the Effects menu. The different types of paper offered in the Painter library can be used, or the desired paper type can be scanned and used. Alternatively, the Make Paper function in the Art Materials palette can be used to design the user's own unique paper, which can then be saved in the library for future use.

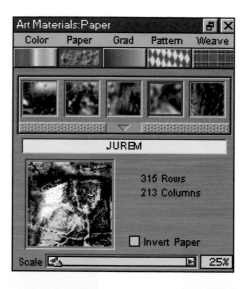

Texture Effects 2

In addition to retouching images for texture, Painter can also be used to create alpha channels for use in Photoshop. This was the technique used to add texture to the outline of the "Eye" image for Project 2. The texture used in this image was created as a black and white image directly in Painter and loaded into an alpha channel in Photoshop. Let's take a closer look.

STEP 1

First we checked the size of the eye image so we can match it in the Painter image.

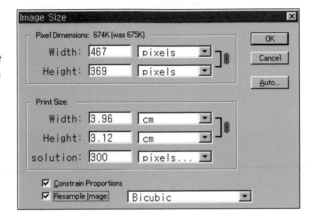

STEP 2

We created a new file, larger than the source image, in Painter. We set the color of the paper to black so that it can be used in Photoshop's channel later.

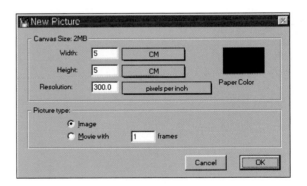

STEP 3

We specified the Paper and set the Brush to Charcoal.

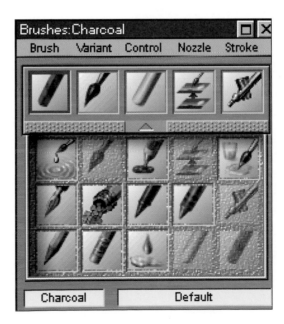

STEP 4

We set the paint color to white and adjusted the size of the brush.

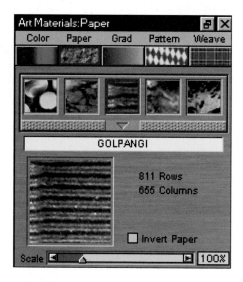

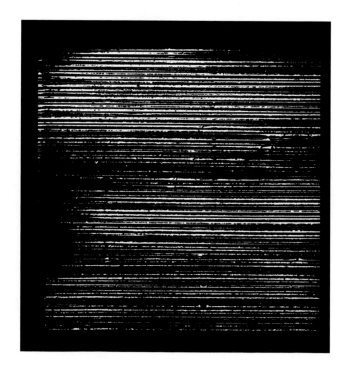

STEP 5

Keeping in mind that this image will be used as a channel in Photoshop later, we made sure that our brush strokes didn't extend past the area that the eye will take up. Then we saved the image in TIFF format.

STEP 6

We started up Photoshop and opened Project 2. Then we opened the black and white image created in Painter. We selected the entire black and white texture and copied it. Returning to Project 2, we created a new channel and pasted the Painter image into it. We converted the channel into a selection in which the white areas of the channel were selected. Then we created a new layer and used the Fill command to place white in the selected area.

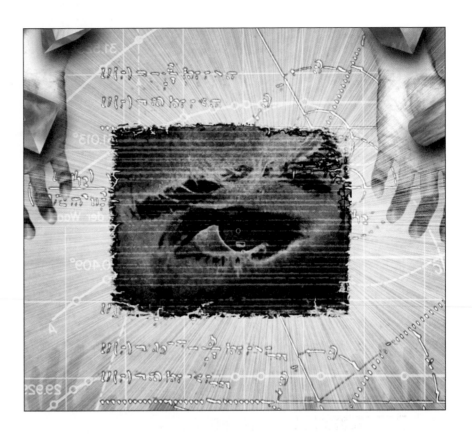

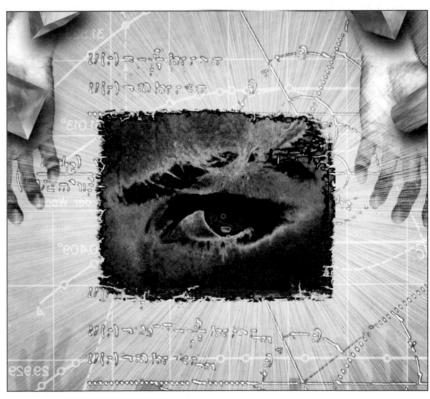

Art Gallery

This is my work.

Complete Agreement.

Complete Agreement. This License constitutes the entire agreement between the parties with respect to the use of the Apple Software, related documentation and fonts, and supersedes all prior or contemporaneous understandings or agreements, written or oral, regarding such subject matter. No amendment to or modification of this License will be binding unless in writing and signed by a duly authorized representative of Apple.